Financial Crisis, Austerity, and Electoral Politics

This book examines the domestic electoral consequences of the economic and financial crisis in Europe, particularly in those countries where the crisis manifested itself more devastatingly: the Southern European countries of Greece, Italy, Portugal, and Spain, as well as Iceland and Ireland. On the surface, the electoral consequences of the crisis seem largely similar, having resulted, in these countries, in large electoral losses for incumbents, as the most elementary versions of "economic voting" theory would have us expect. However, behind this fundamental similarity, important differences emerge. Whilst in some cases, on the basis of post-election surveys, it is possible to see that the "crisis elections" followed a previous pattern of performance-oriented voters, with no major changes either in known predictors of electoral choices or in basic party system properties, other elections brought the emergence of new parties, new issues and cleavages, altering patterns of political competition.

By examining these different outcomes and comparing the "crisis elections" with previous ones, this book takes into account their timing relative to different stages of crisis. It also scrutinises party strategies and campaign dynamics, particularly as governments attempted (and sometimes succeeded) in framing events and proposals so as to deflect responsibility for economic outcomes.

This book was originally published as a special issue of the *Journal of Elections, Public Opinion and Parties.*

Pedro C. Magalhães is Principal Researcher in the Institute of Social Sciences at the University of Lisbon, Portugal. His research interests include public opinion, voting behaviour, political attitudes, and judicial politics.

Financial Crisis, Austerity, and Electoral Politics

European Voter Responses to the Global Economic Collapse 2009–2013

Edited by
Pedro C. Magalhães

Routledge
Taylor & Francis Group

LONDON AND NEW YORK

First published 2015 by Routledge

2 Park Square, Milton Park, Abingdon, Oxon OX14 4RN
711 Third Avenue, New York, NY 10017, USA

Routledge is an imprint of the Taylor & Francis Group, an informa business

First issued in paperback 2017

British Library Cataloguing in Publication Data
A catalogue record for this book is available from the British Library

ISBN 13: 978-1-138-85678-3 (hbk)
ISBN 13: 978-1-138-06157-6 (pbk)

Typeset in Times New Roman
by RefineCatch Limited, Bungay, Suffolk

Publisher's Note
The publisher accepts responsibility for any inconsistencies that may have
arisen during the conversion of this book from journal articles to book chapters,
namely the possible inclusion of journal terminology.

Disclaimer
Every effort has been made to contact copyright holders for their permission to
reprint material in this book. The publishers would be grateful to hear from any
copyright holder who is not here acknowledged and will undertake to rectify
any errors or omissions in future editions of this book.

Contents

Citation Information

The chapters in this book were originally published in the *Journal of Elections, Public Opinion and Parties*, volume 24, issue 2 (May 2014). When citing this material, please use the original page numbering for each article, as follows:

Chapter 5

The Incumbent Electoral Defeat in the 2011 Spanish National Elections: The Effect of the Economic Crisis in an Ideological Polarized Party System
Mariano Torcal
Journal of Elections, Public Opinion and Parties, volume 24, issue 2 (May 2014)
pp. 203–221

Chapter 6

Dealignment, De-legitimation and the Implosion of the Two-Party System in Greece: The Earthquake Election of 6 May 2012
Eftichia Teperoglou & Emmanouil Tsatsanis
Journal of Elections, Public Opinion and Parties, volume 24, issue 2 (May 2014)
pp. 222–242

Chapter 7

The Political Consequences of Blame Attribution for the Economic Crisis in the 2013 Italian National Election
Paolo Bellucci
Journal of Elections, Public Opinion and Parties, volume 24, issue 2 (May 2014)
pp. 243–263

Please direct any queries you may have about the citations to
clsuk.permissions@cengage.com

Notes on Contributors

Paolo Bellucci is Professor of Comparative Political Behaviour in the Centre for the Study of Political Change, University of Siena, Italy.

Indridi H. Indridason is Associate Professor in the Department of Political Science, University of California, Riverside, CA, USA.

Pedro C. Magalhães is Principal Researcher in the Institute of Social Sciences at the University of Lisbon, Portugal.

Michael Marsh is a Fellow Emeritus in the Department of Political Science at Trinity College Dublin, Ireland.

Slava Mikhaylov is a Senior Lecturer in Research Methods in the Department of Political Science at University College London, UK.

Eftichia Teperoglou is a Faculty Member in the Zentrum für Europäische Sozialforschung (MZES) at the University of Mannheim, Germany.

Mariano Torcal is Professor of Political Science at the Universitat Pompeu Fabra, Barcelona, Spain.

Emmanouil Tsatsanis is a Researcher in the Centre for Research and Studies in Sociology at the University Institute of Lisbon, Portugal.

EDITOR'S NOTE

We are pleased to present this issue of JEPOP which is a special issue on the topic of how the financial crisis in Europe has changed the electoral politics of some of the most deeply affected countries. We are delighted to welcome on board Pedro C. Magalhães as guest co-editor for this issue. Pedro is principal researcher at the Institute of Social Sciences of the University of Lisbon, Portugal, and one of the coordinators of the Portuguese Election Study. Pedro is not only the author of one of the articles in this issue but has been instrumental in recruiting the other authors whose work is included, and who originally delivered early versions of these articles at a conference organised by the Department of Government and the BMW Center for German and European Studies of Georgetown University. All articles in this issue have been through JEPOP's rigorous reviewing process and we would like to thank our two referees, Professor Jack Vowles and Professor Sara Hobolt (who waive their anonymity).

Ed Fieldhouse, Mark Franklin and Rachel Gibson

Introduction – Financial Crisis, Austerity, and Electoral Politics

PEDRO C. MAGALHÃES

University of Lisbon, Portugal

The Great Recession has manifested itself in particularly troubling ways in the European continent. In almost all European economies, stagnation in 2008 was followed by an acute GDP contraction the following year. Only by the end of 2011 had the average GDP per capita in the EU 27 recovered to pre-crisis levels, although growth has remained at best sluggish and employment levels have as yet shown little sign of recovery. Indeed, in comparison with previous recessions in 1974–

1976 and 1979–1982, only inflation seems to have posed less of a problem. While the effects of the economic crisis for the Euro-zone and wider world economy have been unquestionably severe, the political consequences are less immediately obvious. It is the linkage between the recent economic crisis and political outcomes in six of those nations most affected by the Great Recession that this issue seeks to explore. Models of vote choice tend to focus on a few major factors, including evaluations of incumbent performance, positions on economic and non-economic issues, and generic non-policy factors (such as party attachments or loyalties – Hellwig, 2008: 1128). If ever there was a time when we would expect performance considerations to become paramount, one would expect it to be in the aftermath of the financial tsunami that engulfed several democracies over the past decade. But to what extent was that the case? Was it a simple equation of voters punishing incumbents for the financial meltdown? Or was the situation more complex? Has the singular nature of this crisis affected judgments about whom to blame for it? Has the relevance of long-standing divisions about economic policies increased or decreased? Have voter loyalties remain strong despite their misgivings about the government's performance?

While most European nations felt the pain of the economic crisis, some experienced it more acutely than others. By the end of 2012, Iceland, Ireland, Greece, Portugal, Spain, and Italy in particular had not seen their economies recover to pre-crisis levels. Only Iceland preserved a rate of unemployment below the European average, while Greece and Spain were already above 25%. In all of these six countries the problems spiraled out beyond the traditional concerns of unemployment, inflation and GDP growth to encompass wider and more complex issues of budget deficits and public debt. Terms such as "bond yield spreads," "credit default swaps" or "CDS," "junk bonds," and "rating agencies," that were previously confined to the world of financiers, became part of the everyday language of journalists, media commentators, and politicians. Ultimately the problems of rising private and public debt levels that they they faced brought them to the brink of financial insolvency during what has become known as the Great Recession.

Despite sharing an extreme manifestation of the global economic crisis, the causes of the economic collapse were not always the same in the six countries. In Iceland and Ireland, the crisis was brought about by a breakdown of the banking system, itself the result of deep bank regulation problems, the bursting of real estate bubbles, and the freezing of interbank markets following the Lehman Brothers bankruptcy. In Iceland, an IMF-led rescue package was agreed in November 2008, one month after the three major banks were placed into receivership. In Ireland, the EU/IMF bailout came two years later, in November 2010. In Greece and Portugal, excessive public spending, low competitiveness and productivity, and the absence of a coordinated response at the domestic and European levels all combined to undermine market confidence, leading to rising spreads on government bonds, their own banking crises, and, ultimately, the inability to meet debt obligations without financial bailouts. These ultimately took place in May 2010 in Greece and one year later in Portugal. By mid 2011, the specter of insolvency had also spread to Italy and Spain, with rising debt service costs in these two very large economies ultimately forcing a much more decisive action of the part of European institutions, including the provision of rescue loans to Spanish banks and, ultimately, the conversion of the European Central Bank into a lender of last resort in sovereign bond markets.[1]

The task of investigating the various causes of the debt crises endured by these countries as well as their short and longer-term economic and social consequences is still ongoing. As noted above, however, the task of this special issue is to better understand their *political*, and more specifically *electoral*, consequences. Before moving on to the detail of the articles' content and key findings, we begin with some *a priori* expectations about the political effects of the Great Recession drawn from the extant literature.

One obvious starting assumption would be that those parties seen as having presided over the economic tumult would be punished for it, particularly within the countries that were most acutely and protractedly affected by the crisis. Such an expectation is based on the relatively simple electoral and political equation that "good times keep parties in office, bad times cast them out" (Lewis-Beck & Stegmaier, 2000: 183). This premise stems from the wider "economic voting" literature which argues that in essence voters judge incumbents retrospectively on the basis of observed performance. If this is the case then it is hard to imagine how election outcomes in these countries could have resulted in anything other than very large punishments for incumbents. In addition to presiding over the severe economic shock delivered by the global financial crisis, the governing parties in these countries faced further humiliation in terms of declaring state insolvency and receiving international financial rescue packages (Iceland, Greece, Ireland, and Portugal) or the very clear threat of these outcomes (Italy and Spain).

On the face of it the facts would seem to support the simple retrospective voting hypothesis. In Iceland, the conservative Independence Party, which had been in power for almost two decades, experienced in 2009 its worst electoral performance in legislative elections since World War II. In Ireland, Fianna Fáil, the historically dominant party in Irish politics, was left in third place in the 2011 elections. In Portugal and Spain, the 2011 elections resulted in major losses for the incumbent Socialist parties and their replacement by center-right governments. In Greece, the post-bailout elections of 2012 led to massive losses for what was once the main center-left party, the Socialist PASOK. In Italy, elections were not even necessary to oust the incumbent. By November 2011, the economic crisis has become so severe and the credibility of the Italian government so tarnished that, as the majority center-right coalition disaggregated, Prime Minister Berlusconi was led to resign. All this seems to vindicate a general reading of the consequences of the Great Recession in Europe: "in periods of economic crisis, as in more normal times, voters have a strong tendency to support any policies that seem to work, and to punish leaders regardless of their ideology when economic growth is slow" (Bartels, 2012: 50). That the punishments of incumbents were so often extreme is, from this point of view, mainly a function of the equally extreme nature of the crises, which affected these economies and governments led by either center-right (Ireland, Iceland, Italy) or center-left (Portugal, Greece, Spain) incumbent parties.

Taking a deeper look at these electoral outcomes, however, as the articles in this issue do, we find that a number of important differences emerge. Voter decisions are rarely based entirely on economic outcomes and the perceived competence of parties in terms of crisis management. We know from well established sources in the extensive electoral behavior literature that parties' and voters' positions on economic and social welfare policies, such as the role of the state in redistributing wealth through taxation and the appropriate level and goals of public spending, are important considerations in the vote calculus. It is true that one of the features of this crisis was that, unlike in previous world recessions, it was met with a remarkably uniform succession of policy responses across countries: first stimulus, then austerity (Pontusson & Raess, 2012). However, the austerity policies unveiled in the six countries under analysis here went beyond traditional "belt tightening" measures adopted by governments and it would be surprising if they failed to intensify divisions among parties and voters. Furthermore, the timing of their introduction in terms of their proximity to or from a national election and the extent of partisan support behind them varied considerably. As such we would expect them to exert a significant moderating effect on the "blame the incumbent" equation set out by the economic voting models.

Further muddying the economic voting waters is the recognition that not all nations and indeed elections are created equal in terms of the extent of "clarity of responsibility" that voters face in assigning incumbents credit or blame for economic and other outcomes. This makes passing judgment about incumbent competence and complicity problematic. Although much of the literature on this subject has focused on the institutional sources of clarity (Powell & Whitten, 1993), the level of economic integration that nations now experience is increasingly seen as an important factor in determining the extent to which citizens can actually be expected to hold governments to account (Kayser, 2007). In the context of the Great Recession and the sovereign debt crisis, which have arguably highlighted the deep integration of the international economy more than ever before, this theme gains a particular relevance. Throughout the last few years, voters have been bombarded with media and partisan messages about international financial contagion and the effects of the behavior of rating agencies, domestic and foreign banks, and European institutions on the domestic economy. Recent research has determined that assignments of responsibility in such a context may matter for vote choices (Hellwig & Coffey, 2011; Lobo & Lewis-Beck, 2012). It has even been argued that, in electoral contexts where the capacity of governments to pursue alternative economic policies is perceived as constrained by exogenous conditions, voters may end up turning to "non-economic" issues such as minority rights, law and order, abortion, the environment, and immigration in order to decide how to cast their vote (Hellwig, 2008). To what extent has the "systemic" ("European" or even "global") nature of the crisis affected voters' sense that blame in fact can be assigned for the disasters endured in the domestic economies of these six countries? Did incumbents succeed in convincing voters that the causes and most drastic consequences of the crisis were beyond their control? Did the economic crisis ironically increase the role of "non-economic" issues?

The articles included in this special issue utilize a range of national and comparative data sources and methods to unpack and interrogate these questions and explanatory models. Taking the cases of Iceland, Ireland, and Portugal, here we see countries where the apex of the economic and financial crisis was most quickly followed by the loss of parliamentary support for governments and an immediate judgment by voters. In Iceland, Prime Minister Haarde resigned in January 2009 and elections were called for May of that year, just a few months after the collapse of the banking sector. In Ireland, the election took place in February 2011, three months after the bailout. In Portugal, the election was in June 2011, just a month after the government requested financial rescue from the Troika formed by the European Commission, the International Monetary Fund and the European Central Bank.

Despite sharing most of the pain of the Great Recession and its immediate political fallout, closer inspection indicates that basic continuities were maintained in the patterns of electoral politics in these three countries. This is most clearly seen in Michael Marsh's and Slava Mikhaylov's article on the 2011 Irish election in this issue, tellingly titled "A conservative revolution." The authors' relentless pursuit of signs of change in individuals' electoral behavior yields very slim pickings. They are left to conclude that: "the 2011 election looks much like that of 2002 and 2007 ... FF lost because it and its leaders were seen to have done a very poor job, and FG, and Labour were a better bet for the future, the converse of 2002 and 2007". Election outcomes aside, there were also few signs of any significant change in the role played by partisan cleavages and policy preferences, particularly around issues of taxation and spending (conceivably more salient in a context of anticipated austerity policies). As the authors put it: "there is little to suggest any of those issues we typically see as providing the substance of left/right debate, at least as measured here, had much impact on voting choice and no sign that they had more effect in 2011".

The accounts of Iceland and Portugal argue a similar case to that put forward for Ireland. In his article on the 2011 Portuguese elections, Pedro Magalhães stresses how, in spite of a somewhat increased polarization of party discourses on economic and welfare policy issues, such issues were, if anything, even less important than in the two previous elections. Instead, and even more so than in 2002 and 2005, elections were "mostly about government performance". Similarly, in Iceland, the 2009 election was largely a "normal" one: as Indridi Indridason notes, and like in previous elections, evaluation of "government performance generally has the expected effect in all three elections [2003, 2007, and 2009] and has become slightly more important over time".

To be sure, there were also some notable differences between these countries. In Iceland and Ireland, blame for the crisis seems to have been placed by most voters squarely on the domestic actors (government and its parties) or institutions that were supposed to have been better controlled and regulated by those governments (banks and financial authorities). In contrast, in Portugal, the assignment of blame for the crisis to incumbent Socialists coexisted with responsibilities also being assigned to agents such as the European Union and rating agencies or even impersonal forces such "the international economic situation," something that seems to have served to partially exonerate the government. There are even signs that, in Portugal, as Hellwig (2008) suggested in his study of France, this context of perceived constraints in the management of the economy was accompanied by a revived importance of non-economic issues. However, what these elections had in common is more important than what separates them; dramatic as the defeat of the incumbents may have been, the elections were, after all, mostly about sanctioning the incumbent and rewarding the main alternatives. This can be seen not only in terms of the prevalence of valence politics or "performance voting" that many have detected in the politics of Western democracies, but also in terms of the concrete aftermath of each election. In Iceland, as Indridason notes, "what is surprising is that the crisis has not affected the political landscape in a more significant way": "the four major parties remain the main political actors". As we now know, the Independence Party even recovered its role as the largest party in the April 2013 elections and found its way back into the government. In Ireland, "the crisis did not result in a redefinition of the electoral landscape" and although "FF's dominance is unlikely to be repeated," current polling at the time of this writing already shows that Fianna Fáil has recovered significant ground. In Portugal, the fundamental properties of the party system, in terms of fragmentation and its five main party players, remained mostly untouched. The center-left party ousted from government, the Socialists, remained the main opposition party, and has regained, since late 2012, a leading position in the voting intention polls.

Discussing the case of Iceland, Indridason precisely notes that "the early election meant that there was very limited time for the dissatisfaction with the political parties to congeal in the form of new political forces capable of challenging the existing parties". This was precisely the opposite of what happened in two other cases analyzed in this special issue, Greece and Italy. There, the onset of the economic and financial crisis was not followed by elections. Instead, sooner (Italy) or later (Greece), what followed was the formation of "national unity" governments, explicitly or tacitly supported by the largest parties in parliament, which then pursued the austerity policies imposed following financial collapse (Greece) or its vivid threat (Italy).

The consequences, as described in the articles on Greece and Italy in this special issue, were ultimately much more dramatic than in the other cases discussed in this special issue. In the 2012 elections in Greece, what Emmanouil Tsatsanis and Eftichia Teperoglou depict is, in their telling words, no less than "the implosion" of the two-party system. It is a collapse visible both on the surface and behind it. On the surface, it includes the spectacular drop in the share of the vote for the two major parties before the crisis. PASOK, the ruling party following the previous 2009 election, took the hardest hit, but ND, which had supported the "national unity" government since November 2011, was deeply affected too. Together with the spectacular rise of SYRIZA, this brought one of the highest levels of electoral volatility ever recorded in a European democracy. Behind the surface, Tsatsanis and Teperoglou show us even more telling signs: a decline in party identification, particularly among the younger voters, rendering them "available" to be mobilized by new parties; a decline in indicators of system support, including satisfaction with democracy and trust in parliament; and the remarkably sharp partisan divides that seem to have been created between voters as the austerity program progressed. These divides were created not only around positions on the economic policies pursued under the Troika, but also around positions vis-à-vis the European Union, immigration control, church–state relations, and even generic attitudes towards political action and the political system. For a country that, by the beginning of the twenty-first century, could be aptly described as experiencing a "trend toward moderation and away from the polarizing logic of the past" (Gunther & Montero, 2001: 150), this was a momentous transformation. Tsatsanis and Teperoglou suggest that the roots of such "moderation" were also, after all, behind its demise. The social bases of the two main Greek parties had been patiently built through large-scale clientelism and patronage appointments to the public sector following each alternation in power, leading to the constant swelling of public administration. However, "the explosion of the fiscal time bomb" and the ensuing austerity policies, by short-circuiting this fundamentally collusive system, "clipped the opportunities for patron-age appointments . . . undermining to a large extent the 'clientelist' social contract that legitimized and reproduced two-party rule in Greece".

In Italy, as Paolo Bellucci's article shows, the story was also one of important electoral change. True, as in Iceland, Ireland, or Portugal, Italian citizens' opinions regarding the performance of government and the economy did matter quite significantly for the vote. However, the way this played out in terms of partisan support was rather different. Monti's period of "technocratic" government, initially supported by a Grand Coalition from which the previous "partisan incumbent" (Berlusconi's PdL) ultimately managed to distance itself strategically, seems to have disturbed normal patterns of accountability and alternation. In spite of the weakened credibility of Berlusconi as prime minister, his PdL, rather than being punished by those who grieved Italy's economic situation and policies, was largely able to evade direct accountability in the 2013 elections. Instead, it was the main alternative, the center-left PD, that was awkwardly left behind to be associated with – and punished by – the economic situation faced by voters just before the election and the austerity policies implemented by Monti. Most strikingly, as Belluci notes, the syndrome of distrust in political parties and gen-eralized political disaffection that characterized Italy, and whose electoral conse-quences had been suppressed since 1994 by the constant alternation in power of the center-right and the center-left, was reawakened and made particularly conse-quential in these circumstances. It was Beppe Grillo's Five Star Movement that emerged as the main beneficiary of voters' mistrust vis-à-vis established political parties, in an election where both the PdL and PD arrived for different reasons, largely delegitimized as alternatives.

Our last case, Spain, is perhaps the most ambivalent of the lot. On the one hand, basic electoral behavior patterns seem quite similar to those that occurred in Iceland, Ireland, and Portugal. As Mariano Torcal's article shows, evaluations of the economy, and especially of the performance of the incumbent party in managing the economy, had a powerful and predictable effect: the worse they were, the more deserted and punished the incumbent PSOE. However, a deeper look shows that "performance voting" was significantly moderated by voters' prior ideological predispositions. For voters located on the right, evaluations of the government's performance in managing the economy were of little relevance. Instead, it was among voters located in the center and on the left that the punishment of PSOE was most related to performance evaluations. Ideology and performance thus interacted in important ways. While PSOE's last two years of incumbency were spent implementing austerity policies that alienated centrist and leftist voters, and were in any case insufficient to address the crisis, PP remained perceived by a large segment of voters to be too far to the right. Thus, in Spain, a country where ideological divisions among voters are profound, the disappointment of voters in the left and center was channeled by switching in unprecedented numbers to, respectively, the Izquierda Unida and UPyD, rather than engrossing the ranks of the PP. Economic crisis, rather than simply causing the replacement of the incumbent with the main alternative on the other side of the political spectrum, also brought about an increased level of party system fragmentation which, at the time of this writing, and on the basis of published polls, risks becoming the "new normal" of this once solid "two-and-a-half" party system.

Surely, at a high level of abstraction, the elections of the Great Recession may indeed have something in common with each other and with many past elections: "good times keep parties in office, bad times cast them out." However, the main lesson that emerges from the study of these six elections is that economic conditions interact with political events, campaign strategies, and economic policies in very consequential ways. In some cases, this produced elections where basic patterns of electoral behavior were preserved and party systems retained most of their fundamental features. In others, this turned elections into profoundly transformative events, that changed the face of electoral and party politics as we knew them in these countries. This is the story that the six articles in this special issue tell in a detailed and fascinating way.

Acknowledgements

This special issue began as a series of papers presented at an April 2012 conference entitled "Political Consequences of the Economic Crisis: Voting and Protesting in Europe since 2008," a joint event of the Department of Government and the BMW Center for German and European Studies of Georgetown University, co-organized by Josep Colomer and myself. This conference was supported by the Luso-American Foundation for Development (FLAD) and by Fundación Endesa, to whom I would like to express my gratitude, as well as to the Department of Government and the BMW Center and to the editors of the *Journal of Elections, Public Opinion and Parties*.

Note

1. For analyses of these developments, see, for example, De Grauwe (2011) and Armingeon and Baccaro (2012).

References

Armingeon, K. & Baccaro, L. (2012) The sorrows of young euro: policy responses to the sovereign debt crisis, in: N. Bermeo & K. Armingeon (eds) *Coping with Crisis: Government Reactions to the Great Recession* (New York: Russell Sage Foundation), pp. 162–198.

Bartels, L. (2012) Elections in hard times. *Public Policy Research*, 19(1), pp. 44–50.

De Grauwe, P. (2011) The governance of a fragile Eurozone. *Revista de Economía Institucional*, 13(25), pp. 33–41.

Gunther, R. & Montero, J.R. (2001) The anchors of partisanship: a comparative analysis of voting behavior in four Southern European democracies, in: P.N. Diamandouros & R. Gunther (eds) *Parties, Politics and Democracy in the New Southern Europe* (Baltimore: Johns Hopkins University Press), pp. 83–152.

Hellwig, T. (2008) Globalization, policy constraints, and vote choice. *The Journal of Politics*, 70(4), pp. 1128–1141.

Hellwig, T. & Coffey, E. (2011) Public opinion, party messages, and responsibility for the financial crisis in Britain. *Electoral Studies*, 30(3), pp. 417–426.

Kayser, M.A. (2007) How domestic is domestic politics? Globalization and elections. *Annual Review of Political Science*, 10, pp. 341–362.

Lewis-Beck, M.S. & Stegmaier, M. (2000) Economic determinants of electoral outcomes. *Political Science*, 3(1), p. 183.

Lobo, M.C. & Lewis-Beck, M.S. (2012) The integration hypothesis: how the European Union shapes economic voting. *Electoral Studies*, 31(3), pp. 522–528.

Pontusson, J. & Raess, D. (2012) How (and why) is this time different? The politics of economic crisis in western Europe and the United States. *Annual Review of Political Science*, 15, pp. 13–33.

Powell Jr, G.B. & Whitten, G.D. (1993) A cross-national analysis of economic voting: taking account of the political context. *American Journal of Political Science*, 37(2), pp. 391–414.

The Collapse: Economic Considerations in Vote Choice in Iceland

INDRIDI H. INDRIDASON
University of California – Riverside, Riverside, USA

ABSTRACT *This paper examines the consequences of the collapse of the Icelandic banking system in the fall of 2008 on voters' support for the political parties. The literature on economic voting has demonstrated that voters hold governments accountable for past economic outcomes, and such concerns should be especially salient in times of large-scale economic crisis such as that experienced by Iceland. In such cases, where the cause is more likely to be seen as the consequence of policies having to do with organization of the economy and, in particular the banking sector, rather than a consequence of short term economic management, the question of who voters hold accountable is of particular interest.*

1 Introduction

The quick onset of the economic crises in Iceland in 2008 was perhaps its defining feature. While it would be an exaggeration to say that things fell apart overnight, it wouldn't be all that far from the truth. In the span of a few days Iceland's three largest banks were placed into receivership and every day appeared to bring a new batch of bad news.[1] Icelanders felt the consequences of the collapse of the banking system immediately. People who had invested in the banks' stocks saw their savings wiped out. While perhaps not significant in itself there was no way to get money in or out of the country for a few days, which bred feelings of isolation and helplessness among many. Most importantly, the banking crisis was accompanied by a significant devaluation of the Icelandic krona. On October 8, 2008 a dollar traded for 126 krona – a year earlier the exchange rate was 60 krona to the dollar. While a fall in the value of a currency has substantial effects on consumption in countries that really heavily on imports, there were additional complications in the Icelandic case. Interest rates had been kept very high in Iceland and, as a consequence, taking out mortgages and other loans in foreign currency – at substantially lower rates – had become quite common. The devaluation of the Icelandic krona meant that many people faced mortgage payments twice what they had been at the origination of the mortgage – in effect, the principal now far exceeded the value of the properties. This, along with restriction on the ability to trade currencies freely, also meant that for a little while Iceland became a net exporter of luxury cars – without any production of cars taking place in Iceland.

The crisis also had substantial political consequences. People took to the streets in protest against the government of the Independence Party and the Social Democratic Alliance and its handling of the financial crisis in what become known as the Kitchenware Revolution. In January 2009, prime minister Haarde announced his retirement from politics for health reasons and that an early election would be called in May. The coalition parties were unable to reach an agreement about who would lead the government in place of Haarde. The Independence Party's insistence that the new prime minister would come from the ranks of the Independence Party, and the Social Democrats' unwillingness to accept that, eventually lead to the dissolution of the government. The government was replaced by a minority government of the Socials Democratic Alliance and the Left Movement that was protected against a vote of no confidence by the Progressive Party and the Liberal Party. The coalition government agreed that an early election would be held on April 25, 2009.

The 2009 parliamentary election was contested by seven parties. In addition to the five parties that were represented in the legislature at the time,[2] two new parties presented candidates. The Citizens' Movement was founded by various grassroots movements that formed after the collapse of the banks and was essentially a protest party that campaigned on issues of democratic reforms, equality, and radical solutions to the problems facing households in the wake of the crisis. The Democratic Movement campaigned on issues of democratic reform and, in particular, demands for direct democracy. The outcome of the election altered the political landscape considerably. The Independence Party was the big loser of election, losing 13% of the vote. The Progressive Party, the Independence Party's coalition partner from 1995 to 2007, gained 3% pts. over the previous election for an additional two seats in parliament (out of 63). The Social Democratic Alliance made some advances, gaining two seats, while the Left Movement and the Citizen's Movement were the winners of the election, each posting a gain of over 7% of the vote from the previous election and winning an additional, respectively, five and four seats in the legislature. The Social Democratic Alliance and the Left Movement, who had governed as a minority coalition since the dissolution of the Independence Party and the Social Democratic Alliance coalition earlier in the year, renewed their coalition, now supported by a legislative majority, on May 10, 2009.

In terms of examining how economic crises affect electoral outcomes, Iceland is an interesting case for several reasons. First, it offers an opportunity to examine whether, and if so how, voters hold parties accountable for the state of the economy. As in the other articles in this volume, the question is whether voters focus on governments' past success in managing the economy or on prospective, or ideological, evaluations of the parties in times of economic stress. There is a well-established body of work dating back to Key (1966) that demonstrates that retrospective evaluations of economic performance influence voters' decisions in a fairly straightforward manner while more recent contributions have emphasized factors such as clarity of responsibility condition economic voting (Powell & Whitten, 1993) and how economic evaluations shape prospective evaluations of parties (Duch & Stevenson, 2008). More significant shocks to the economy may, possibly, trigger a different response from voters. It has been observed that left governments have become a rarity in the wake of the recession, suggesting that voters have rejected the luxurious welfare policies of the left in favor of the right's greater perceived competence in economic matters.[3] Bartels (2011, 2012), examining the question of whether voters adopt a retrospective view, holding incumbents accountable, or a prospective view, in this case favoring the ideological right, concludes that voters focus more on the incumbents' performance than their ideological orientation. Iceland is a particular interesting case for examining these questions as the incumbent government had only taken the reins of power a year and half prior to the election. Thus, it is difficult to argue that the government at the time of the crises was fully responsible for the crises. Examining the extent to which voters held these parties responsible, therefore, offers an insight into the degree to which voters make 'reasoned' decisions about who to hold accountable and the degree to which they act impulsively in reaction to their economic situation.

Second, the major party in the incumbent IP-SDA coalition had been in government since 1991. One might, therefore, expect voters to assign more of the blame to the IP as it was both in government during the time at which the Icelandic banks were privatized and grew rapidly at the time of the banks' collapse. Third, Iceland speaks to the question of whether responses to an economic crisis are based on prospective evaluations about which parties are best capable of managing the economy or retrospective evaluations of past economic performance (or failures). Two things are required to demonstrate that economic crisis leads to the return of right wing parties to power: first, right-wing parties must become more popular and, second, the previous government must have been a government of the left. This, of course, makes it difficult to say whether voters are driven by favorable evaluations of right-wing parties' ability to revive the economy or if they are merely venting their anger on the government of the day. The Icelandic case helps answer this question. Although the government in power at the time of the collapse was a centrist government, the analysis below shows that the voters assigned greater blame for the crises to the right-wing coalition party.

Finally, the economic crisis in Europe has brought out growing tensions between the European Union and individual member states. Iceland is an interesting case in this regard because, unlike the other countries in this volume, it is not a member of the European Union. Moreover, until the collapse, membership in the European Union had never been a salient public issue. However, some of the immediate consequences of the economic crisis – in particular, the direct costs associated with the devaluation of the Icelandic currency – raised questions about whether being a member of the EU and the Euro would have minimized the economic consequences or even changed the course of events.

2 The Importance of the Economic Crisis

Economic issues weighed heavier on Icelanders ahead of the 2009 parliamentary election than in previous elections. As Figure 1 shows, the crisis was quite severe. After years of sustained economic growth, the economy contracted by nearly 7%. Given the magnitude of the crisis, one would expect the economy to have been more salient than in the previous two elections (2003 and 2007) that followed periods of sustained economic growth. The Icelandic National Election Study asks an open-ended question about which two issues the respondent considers most important. While the question has been asked from the beginning of the Icelandic National Election Study, the coding scheme was changed with 2003 study. The responses to the question in the three studies conducted since then are coded into roughly 40 specific categories that are collapsed into a smaller number of categories for clearer presentation.

Figure 2 shows the proportion of respondents that mentioned each of the 16 policy areas as the most and the second most important issue in the three elections. Social Services were considered one of the most important issues and received the highest proportion of total mentions in each election. In 2007 it was clearly the dominant issue whereas in 2003 it was in close contest with economic issues and the fisheries issue, which had to do with the system of fishing quotas. Economic issues hardly played any role in the 2007 election and issues such the environment, the urban-rural divide, and the health care system received about as much attention. The landscape changed drastically in 2009. The economic crisis was the most frequently mentioned issue, followed by social services. However, the figure likely understates the importance of the economic crisis as some respondents cited economic policy, which in many instances was in reference to the crisis without it being explicitly mentioned. The same may be true for those respondents mentioning social services, i.e., in some instances the respondents mentioned the financial situation of households. While the number of respondents mentioning social services is not out of line with

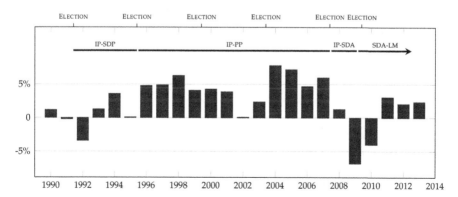

Figure 1. Real GDP growth rate and government composition.
Source: EuroStat

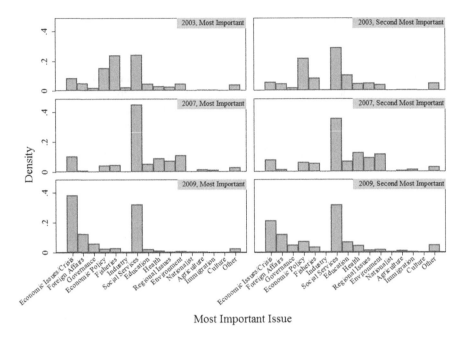

Most Important Issue

Figure 2. Most important election issues.
Source: ICENES 2003–2009.

previous years it appears reasonable to suppose that some of those responses were motivated by issues related to the financial crisis and, in particular, the financial burden imposed on households that had taken out mortgages in foreign currency. Overall, it is safe to say that the economy weighed heavier on voters' minds in 2009 than in previous elections.

Figures 3 and 4 provide further indications that economic concerns played a significant role in 2009.[4] Figure 3 graphs data from Capacent's monthly survey that

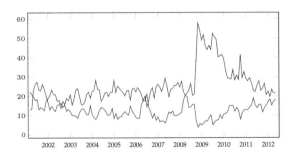

Figure 3. Expectations: household income.
Source: Capacent/Datamarket.com

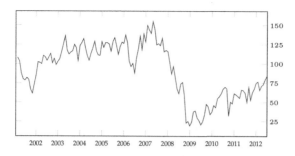

Figure 4. Capacent's consumer confidence index.
Source: Capacent/Datamarket.com.

includes a question about expectations regarding how household income will change in the coming months. The figure shows that there is a sharp increase of respondents that expect household income to fall with a corresponding, albeit smaller, decrease in the number of respondents that expect household income to increase. It is, however, interesting that the expectations had begun to change prior to the collapse in October 2008. The consumer confidence index in Figure 4 tells much the same story. Consumer confidence reached a low following the collapse but began decreasing about a year earlier, most likely due to the weakening of the Icelandic krona.

I begin by exploring the effects of the economy on voters' aggregate support for government. The data come from monthly surveys conducted by Capacent. The data cover the period from May 2001 to February 2012 (with the exception of consumer confidence for which the time series ends in December 2011). The data includes three coalition governments; the coalition of the Independence Party and the Progressive Party formed April 23, 1995 that lasted until the 2007 parliamentary election,[5] the coalition of the Independence Party and the Social Democrats that formed following the 2007 election and the coalition of the Social Democrats and the Left-Green Movement that took office on February 1, 2009 after the collapse of the economy and the dissolution of Haarde's cabinet.[6]

Government support is measured as the percentage of respondents who supported the government (out of those that responded yes or no).[7] The main independent variables are *Consumer Confidence* and *Income Expectations* – or change in the variables when first-differences are modeled. The index of *Consumer Confidence* is calculated by Capacent from five questions about consumer evaluation of current and expected economic conditions.[8] The variable *Income Expectations* is the difference in the percentage of those that expect household income to be higher in six months minus the percentage that think that household income will decrease. In addition to these variables, we include indicator variables for government composition as well as an interaction between the government indicators and the economic expectation variables to allow for different 'baseline' popularity of the different governments as well as the possibility that economic expectations have different effects on the popularity of the different governments. As the two economic expectation variables are highly collinear, separate models are estimated for each of the variables in addition to a model that includes both *Consumer Confidence* and *Income Expectations*. The models also include a *Time Trend* to account for the fact that governments are likely to lose support the longer they stay in office (Strøm, 1984).

The results are presented in Table 1. The results are fairly consistent across the six models presented in the table. The variables measuring economic expectations are estimated to have a positive effect on support for the government but the marginal effect is statistically insignificant in one instance, i.e., the effect of expected income on government support (column 2).[9] The marginal effects of the variables for the different coalitions are shown in Figure 5. There is not much evidence to suggest that the effects of economic expectations depend on the coalition in office. The IP-SDA coalition appears to be disproportionately affected by economic expectations in the first two models where *Government Support* is the dependent variable but there are no statistically significant differences between the coalitions after first differences have been taken. The effect is moderate in magnitude. A one percentage point decline in consumer confidence reduces government support by about 0.08 − 0.1 percentage points. The effect of a unit change in economic expectations appears to be slightly larger, or about 0.13 percentage points. While one must be cautious about interpreting the findings as demonstrating a causal relationship between economic expectations and support for the government, the findings are consistent with the hypothesis that voters hold governments accountable for the state of the economy.

In sum, it is clear that voters were affected by the economic crises and that their economic expectations affect their evaluation of government support but that not all government parties are affected equally. Figure 6 suggests that the Independence Party bore the brunt of the voters' dissatisfaction with the economic crisis. The party lost nearly 13 percentage points at the polls, which amounts to over one-third of its share of the vote in 2007, reaching a historic low. Apart from the minor Liberal Party, the other parties gained votes from the previous election with the Left Movement being the biggest winner gaining 7.4% of the vote.

3   Vote Choice in Times of Crisis

While the aggregate statistics are revealing they do not tell the whole story about what motivated voters to abandon the Independence party in such large numbers and why the Left Movement ended up being the biggest beneficiary. Data from the Icelandic National Election Study are used to examine whether the determinants of vote choice differed in the election that took place following the economic crises compared with the previous two elections (2003 and 2007).

In contrast with the two previous elections, which were held during a period of sustained economic growth, the 2009 election was held only half a year after the onset of the economic crisis. It was, therefore, to be expected that voters would go to the polls with a different set of concerns and, in particular, be more sensitive to issues related to economic conditions. Expectations about the effects of particular variables are

Table 1. Government support and economic expectations

	Gov't Support		Δ Gov't Support			
	(1)	(2)	(3)	(4)	(5)	(6)
Gov't$_{IP\&SDA}$	−23.51***	−2.317	−1.011	−0.913	−1.077	−1.054
	(0.000)	(0.278)	(0.664)	(0.704)	(0.638)	(0.649)
Gov't$_{SDA\&LM}$	−5.255	−14.28***	−1.210	−1.265	−1.201	−1.343
	(0.141)	(0.000)	(0.560)	(0.544)	(0.546)	(0.502)
Consumer Confidence	0.0391					
	(0.201)					
ΔConsumer Confidence			0.0831**	0.0527		
			(0.032)	(0.317)		
Cons. Conf. × Gov't$_{IP\&SDA}$	0.214***					
	(0.000)					
Cons. Conf. × Gov't$_{SDA\&LM}$	−0.115**					
	(0.033)					
Cons. Conf. × Gov't$_{IP\&SDA}$				0.0438		
				(0.669)		
Cons. Conf. × Gov't$_{SDA\&LM}$				0.0823		
				(0.369)		
Expected Income		0.00955				
		(0.895)				
ΔExpected Income					0.132*	0.0513
					(0.052)	(0.630)
Exp. × Gov't$_{IP\&SDA}$		0.363***				
		(0.000)				

(Continued)

Table 1. (Continued)

	Gov't Support		Δ Gov't Support			
	(1)	(2)	(3)	(4)	(5)	(6)
Exp. × Gov't$_{SDA\&LM}$		−0.133				
		(0.116)				
ΔExp. × Gov't$_{IP\&SDA}$						0.0885
						(0.579)
ΔExp. × Gov't$_{SDA\&LM}$						0.191
						(0.254)
Government Support$_{t-1}$	0.537***	0.564***				
	(0.000)	(0.000)				
Time Trend	−0.106***	−0.0831***	−0.00476	−0.00439	−0.00384	−0.00358
	(0.000)	(0.004)	(0.849)	(0.862)	(0.876)	(0.885)
Constant	29.90***	30.77***	0.285	0.273	0.223	0.223
	(0.000)	(0.000)	(0.902)	(0.907)	(0.922)	(0.922)
Observations	124	127	124	124	127	127

p-values in parentheses
* $p < 0.10$, ** $p < 0.05$, *** $p < 0.01$

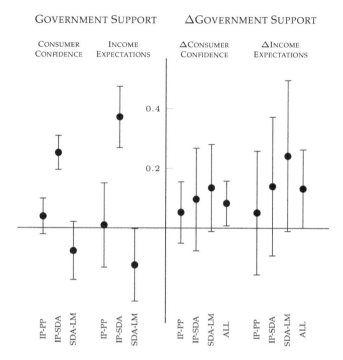

Figure 5. Marginal effects of economic perceptions – by government.

presented below under the headings of (i) the economy and government performance, (ii) European Union membership, and (iii) responsibility, accountability, and political efficacy. Each subsection discusses the results with regard to the variables but before proceeding it is useful to highlight, in a general way, how the economic crisis was likely to shape vote choice. As Iceland was governed by a center-right coalitions (first IP-PP and then IP-SDA) in the years leading up to the economic collapse it represents a particularly interesting case. Perceptions of competence in economic management generally favor the parties of the right while the occurrence of an economic crisis naturally challenges any such claims of competence. Given the difficulty of reconciling these two views, it is reasonable to expect government performance and concern with the economic situation to shape voters' decisions, and that these will tend to favor the SDA and the LM who had been in opposition during most of the period in which the Icelandic banks had grown so rapidly.[10] Some differences are, however, to be expected between the SDA and the LM. The perceived relationship between ideology and economic competence ought to favor the more moderate left party. Similarly, while opinions on EU membership remained divided, the sudden attractiveness of the euro in the face of the devaluation of the krona may have raised the salience of EU membership for some and that change was expected to favor the SDA as the only clear pro-EU option.

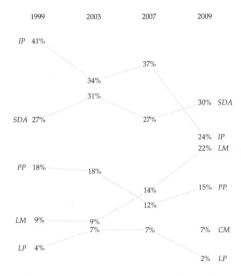

Figure 6. Electoral outcomes 1999–2009.

To analyze determinants of vote choice in the three elections a mixed conditional logit model is used, which allows the examination of the effects of both party and voter characteristics. The analysis is restricted to the parties that won seats in parliament in each election.[11] The models estimated for each election differ slightly as some of the variables of interests were not included in all three surveys. The results of the estimation and details about the control variables not discussed here are given in the appendix. To provide a sense of how the effects of the variables vary across elections, Figure 7 shows the effects of one standard deviation change in the value of the individual specific variables on the predicted probability of a vote for each party.[12] Interpreting whether a particular factor has become more important over the years is not straightforward – for one thing, as one party's gain most be another's loss, the predicted changes in the probability of voting for the different parties must always add up to zero. Thus, to provide summary statistics, the last panel in the figure calculates the sum of the absolute values and the standard deviation of change in predicted probabilities across the parties. Larger values indicate that the variable had a bigger impact on the respondents' choices.

3.1 The Economy and Government Performance

The respondents' views about which party they consider best capable of managing the economy are expected to affect their vote decisions. The variable *Best Party for the Economy* is a dummy variable coded one for parties that respondents identified as the party best capable of managing economic issues and zero for other parties.[13] The salience respondents accorded to the economic situations is also likely to affect voters' choices. If right parties are perceived as being better at managing the

20

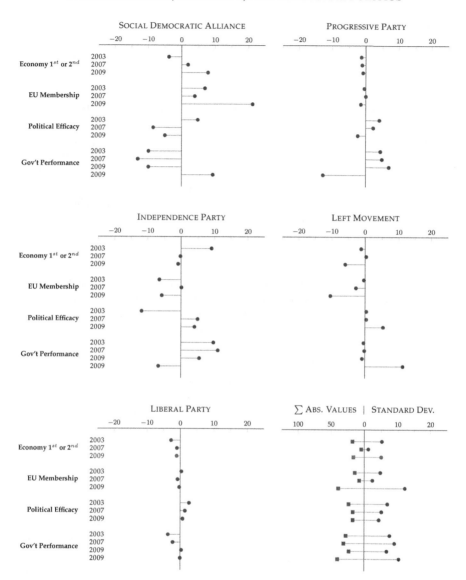

Figure 7. Change in probability of vote – the effect of a one standard deviation change in independent variable.

economy, voters that consider the economy the most salient issue should be more likely to vote for them. As discussed above, whether that is the case in the Icelandic context is not clear as the economic crisis occurred following a prolonged period of center-right governments. However, a conditional ideological economic competency hypothesis can be advanced; the more right-leaning opposition parties are expected to be more likely to receive votes from those concerned about the economy. *Economy 1st or 2nd* is an indicator variable that is coded one if the respondent cited the economy or issues related to it in open ended questions that asked the respondent what they considered the two most important issues to be addressed.

While such prospective evaluations of the parties' policies may matter, they do not operate in isolation. Rather, respondents are likely to also evaluate the parties in light of their past performance and in times of significant economic crisis it appears likely that evaluations of the parties' past performance overshadow the promise of the parties' platforms. The variables *IP-SDA Performance* and *SDA-LM Performance* are the respondents' ratings of the performance of the two government coalitions on a scale from 1 (Very Poor) to 4 (Very Good). Higher scores are expected to increase the likelihood of a vote for the parties in the coalition being evaluated. Ideology is measured on a ten-point left-right scale and *Left-Right Distance* is the absolute difference between the respondent's positions and the party's position.

The results indicate that the economy did indeed play a significant role in vote choice. For the 2009 election, the coefficient for *Best Party for Economy* is large and statistically significant at the 99% level of significance. In substantive terms, the effect of the variable is very large. The average increase in the likelihood of receiving a vote from being considered the best party for the economy (compared with no party being the best party for the economy) is 23.2 percentage points for the IP and 34.7 points for the SDA. The size of the effect suggests that economic considerations were paramount in the election. The question was not asked in the other surveys but the 2007 survey asked which party was considered to have the best tax policy. The effect of being considered the best party on tax policy was 16.5 percentage points for the IP and 17.2 percentage points for the SDA. This suggests that the effect was substantially smaller in 2007 but the differences in the questions obviously limit the inference that can be drawn.

It is not a clear that concerns about the economy had a bigger influence in 2009 than in previous elections. While concerns about the economy had virtually no effect in 2007, the average effect was almost identical in 2003 and 2009. However, there has been a shift in which parties benefit from voters' concern with the economy. In 2003 the IP was more likely to receive votes from voters concerned with the economy but by 2009 the SDA had taken the IP's place. However, voters were significantly less likely to vote for the LM in 2009 – suggesting that left parties do face challenges during times of economic hardship as suggested above. In particular, the SDA appears to gain from concerns about the economy as the least left-leaning party outside of those that had governed in the years leading up to the economic collapse. It is important to note that this comparison doesn't tell the whole story. While being concerned about the economy had about the same propensity to affect a voter's decision in 2009, one must keep in mind that, as shown above, far more voters were concerned about the economy in 2003 and 2007. In other words, individual voters didn't respond more vigorously to their worries about the economy – there were simply more people worried about the economy and, therefore, the economy had a bigger impact than in previous years.

Government Performance generally has the expected effect in all three elections and has only become slightly more important over time.[14] The 2009 election does not stand out in terms of the effect of performance on vote choice. One might note that respondents evaluated two governments in the 2009 survey but, somewhat surprisingly, evaluations of the two governments are not correlated ($r = 0.02$). Again, although individual voters did not react in a significantly stronger manner to *Government Performance* in 2009, those who responded rated the two governments that ruled between 2007 and 2009 significantly worse than the previous government.[15] Of course, endogeneity is a concern here as evaluations of government performance are likely influenced by partisanship but there is little that can be done to solve the problem without more detailed data. It is somewhat counterintuitive that a positive evaluation of the performance of the IP-SDA coalition reduced the probability of voting for the SDA and increased the probability of voting for the PP. One possible explanation is that supporters of the IP and the PP were most likely to believe that the government was not responsible for the crisis. Thus, it is possible that the those that had a more favorable view of the government's performance were also more favorably disposed to the center-right and right parties.

3.2 *The Question of European Union Membership*

The banking crisis led many to re-evaluate their opinion about whether Iceland should join the European Union. Some wondered whether Icelandic citizens might have been spared the pain of the collapse of the Icelandic currency had they joined the EU and adopted the euro. More, however, appear to have considered the Icesave affair, in part, a consequence of European cooperation, and opposition to EU membership rose from 32.4% in August 2008 to 45.5% in February 2009 (Hardarson & Kristinsson, 2010; Capacent, 2011). Voters favoring EU membership are expected to be more likely to vote for the SDA – the only party to favor EU membership. However, prior to the 2009 election the Progressive Party revised its position from being against EU membership to expressing willingness to apply for membership and then deciding for or against membership on the basis of the outcome of the accession negotiation. The expectation is, thus, that voters favoring EU membership are more likely to vote for the SDA and, to a lesser extent, for the PP in the 2009 election. Additionally, as EU membership was likely more salient to voters in 2009 than in previous elections, the effect can be expected to be greater in the 2009 election. To capture the effect of views about EU membership, the variable *Pro EU Membership* is included in the model. *Pro EU Membership* takes values from 0 (strongly against membership) to 4 (strongly for membership).

Attitudes about EU membership clearly had a bigger impact in 2009 than in the previous two elections. As in previous elections, the SDA was more likely to receive votes from pro-EU voters but the size of the effect tripled in 2009 (to +21.2% pts). In 2003, a favorable view of EU membership netted the SDA an additional 6.9% of the vote (primarily at the expense of the IP) but only 3.9% pts. in 2007. The dividing line on EU membership, however, appears to have changed over time with the Left Movement becoming a less favored choice among EU supporters (-10.4% pts. in 2009) although the IP also remained a less preferred option among those voters (-5.8% pts. in 2009). Despite the Left Movement's anti-EU position it went on to form a coalition with the Social Democrats in 2009 and parliament passed a motion to apply for membership to the EU on July 16, 2009. The motion passed with 33 votes against 28 with two MPs abstaining. The Left Movement's MPs split their votes on the motion (8–5) and the motion would not have passed without the support of opposition MPs. The SDA's electoral gains, along with the shift in the PP's attitude towards the EU, can be see as instrumental to Iceland's decision to enter accession negotiations with the EU.[16]

3.3. *Responsibility, Accountability, and Political Efficacy*

The analysis above suggests that voters do not hold all governments accountable for economic performance in the same way and that evaluations of government performance affect vote choice as one would expect. The 2009 election is especially interesting in this regard – both because of the economic context as well as it offering an opportunity to examine how voters allocate responsibility for the crisis among the governing parties. Voters may allocate responsibility in different ways. Hellwig (2008) shows that globalization reduces the degree to which voters hold politicians accountable for economic matters and Hobolt & Tilley (forthcoming) similarly find that voters are sensitive to the institutional constraints politicians face in their study of attribution of responsibility within the EU. Thus, citizens of a small, open economy that is a member of the European Economic Area (EEA) might regard the economic crises to have been brought on by factors outside of control of domestic politicians. This was certainly one of the narratives proposed, i.e., the bankruptcy of the Lehman Brothers set in motion a chain of events that eventually led to the Icelandic banks being placed in receivership and the 'Icesave' deposit debacle being a consequence of Iceland's membership in the EEA that allowed free movement of capital. However, the election results suggest that voters allocate at least some responsibility to domestic political actors but the question then is: "Which parties?" Voters may simply hold the parties on whose watch the economic crisis occurs responsible. Slightly more sophisticated voters may hold the government parties accountable but attribute more of the blame to the party of the prime ministers (Anderson, 2000) – or, alternatively, the party whose ministers occupy key portfolios relevant to the management of the economy, e.g., the ministry of finance (the IP in 2007–2009) and the ministry of commerce (SDA in 2007–2009). Alternatively, voters may have seen the crisis as the results of economic management over a longer period of time. This is somewhat likely to have been the case in Iceland as the country had been governed by an IP–PP coalition for over a decade before the formation of the IP–SDA coalition in 2007. Moreover, the IP–PP coalition had overseen significant privatization – importantly, the privatization of the state banks – during its time in office and lack of regulation and effective oversight of the banking sector is often cited as one of the sources of the economic collapse. Thus, taking a longer view, voters may have held the IP and the PP more accountable than the SDA, which only recently had entered government.

The 2009 Icelandic National Election Study provides an opportunity to address these question as it included a series of questions about who was responsible for the collapse of the banking sector (on a scale from 0 to 10) – in addition to the political parties, these actors included the Central Bank, the Financial Supervisory Authority (FSA), the commercial banks, and Geir H. Haarde's government (IP-SDA). Figure 8 graphs the mean level of responsibility that survey respondents assigned to the different actors. The Financial Supervisory Authority, the Central Bank and the commercial banks are rated as bearing great responsibility but are followed closely by Haarde's government and the Independence Party. The opposition parties, the LM and the LP, are seen as being largely free from responsibility. The SDA, the minor partner in Haarde's coalition government, is considered to bear significantly less responsibility for the banking crisis than the IP despite the fact that the party headed the Ministry of Commerce. This appears consistent with two of the possible explanations offered above. First, the party leading the coalition may be held accountable to a greater degree than the minor party in the coalition. Second, voters may have seen the causes of the banking crisis as something that developed over a longer period of time but the SDA only entered government in May 2007, some 16 months before the banking crisis, whereas the IP had been in government since 1991. The fact that the IP's previous coalition partner, the PP, is considered to bear greater responsibility than the SDA – but less than the IP – suggests that it is a combination of the two explanations. If respondents ignore the history leading up to the banking crisis than they should have rated the PP in a similar way as the LM. The PP is also rated as bearing substantively less responsibility

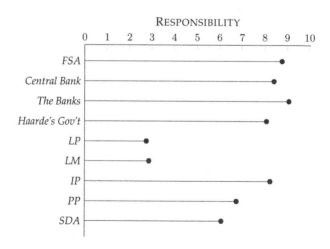

Figure 8. Responsibility for banking crisis

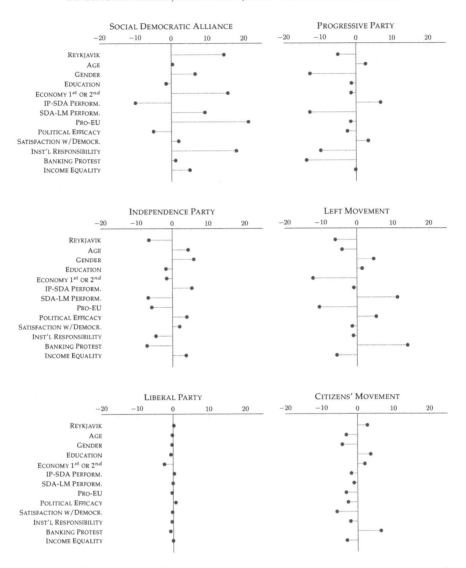

Figure 9. Change in probability of vote – the effect of a one standard deviation change in independent variable

than the IP, which suggests that leadership of the coalition matters – the IP led the parties' coalition for all but 21 months in the period from 1995 to 2007.

Voters are expected to be more likely to vote for the party that they consider less responsible for the crisis. The expectations about respondents that hold non-party actors responsible for the crises are less straightforward. While one might expect responsibility not attributed to the parties to have no effect on the parties' support,

26

Table 2. Responsibility for banking crisis – correlation

	Haarde Gov't	IP	SDA
IP	0.709	—	
SDA	0.414	0.359	—
PP	0.422	0.605	0.245

there is an argument that the Independence Party and the Progressive Party would be affected. Having governed for over a decade prior to the economic crises the two coalition partners could be seen as having created the market conditions that allowed the size of the Icelandic banking system to balloon to unsustainable levels.

Participation in the mass protests following the crises and respondents' sense of political efficacy also tap into views about responsibility and accountability – one of the main demands of the protesters was that the government shoulder responsibility for the crisis. Protesters and those that have expressed a low degree of political efficacy are expected to be more likely to vote for parties that have been excluded from government participation and that advocate political reform. In the 2009 election, the LM and the CM are expected to be more likely to receive support from these groups of voters.

Responsibility for Crisis, the respondents' assessment of each party's responsibility for the economic crisis on a 0–10 scale with 0 indicating no responsibility, was included in the vote choice model for the 2009 election. The variable is coded as zero for the Civic Movement as the party was not represented in parliament until after the 2009 election. The variable *Institutional Responsibility* is the sum of the respondents' answers to the survey questions about how much responsibility the Financial Supervisory Authority, the Central Bank and the commercial banks bore. *Banking Protester* is an indicator variable coded one if the respondent participated in a protest after the banks collapsed in October 2008. A proxy for *Political Efficacy* is the sum of the responses to two questions in the survey that asked respondents to evaluate statements about whether voting and who holds the reins of government matters for political outcomes. The level of agreement with the statements was expressed on a five-point scale with higher numbers indicating that the respondent thought voting/who was in power mattered. Finally, many saw the economic collapse as failure of a political system that was more responsive to special interests than the citizens as a whole. *Satisfaction w/Democracy* is, therefore, expected to affect vote choice with those dissatisfied being more likely to vote for the parties that have less experience in government (the LM and the LP) and, in particular, the new CM, which explicitly campaigned on democratic reform. In *Satisfaction w/Democracy* vote choice is coded from 0 (very dissatisfied) to 4 (very satisfied).

The results indicate that the voters punish those parties that they considered responsible for the crisis although the effect is not extraordinarily large – a one standard deviation change in *Responsibility for Crisis* is predicted to reduce the party vote shares between 2.2% pts. (IP) and 6.4% pts. (SDA).[17] With institutional responsibility, the effects are substantially larger, especially with regard to the SDA, which is far more likely (+17.8% pts.) to receive votes from those that considered the banks and the FSA responsible. In contrast, these voters were less likely to vote for the IP (−4.6% pts) and the PP (−9.9% pts).

Participants in the banking protests were less likely to vote for the parties on the right of the political spectrum. Protesters were more likely to vote for the Left Movement (+14.1% pts) and the Civic Movement (+6.4% pts), and to a smaller degree the Social Democratic Alliance (+1.1% pts). *Political Efficacy* and *Satisfaction w/Democracy* were also found to affect vote choice. The Civic Movement was clearly the party of those disillusioned with the political system (−2.6% pts and −11.4% pts, respectively). Interestingly the centrist parties, the Social Democratic Alliance (−4.9% pts) and the Progressive Party (−2.4% pts), were less likely than the parties on the left and the right to receive votes from voters that have a high degree of *Political Efficacy*. Voters with a high degree of *Satisfaction w/Democracy*, however, were somewhat less likely to vote for the Left Movement (−1.0% pts) although the differences were not statistically significant at the 90% level.

Figure 7 shows the effects of *Political Efficacy* on vote choice for the three elections. Interestingly, *Political Efficacy* appears to have declined in importance over time but there is not a significant shift after the crisis. Of course, the figure shows the effect of *Political Efficacy* and does not speak to the fact of whether voters' sense of political efficacy has increased or declined. That is, it is quite possible that voters' sense of political efficacy had declined from previous elections. However, political efficacy was a weaker predictor of party choice than in previous elections, which, perhaps, is not surprising, as a voter that beliefs that neither their vote nor the candidates they elect matters is likely to have strong preference about who she votes for. The declining effect of *Political Efficacy* is also consistent with Icelanders becoming acutely aware of their small economy being vulnerable to external circumstances and with a declining trust in politicians and political institutions in general.

4   Conclusions

The collapse of the Icelandic banking sector and the economic crisis that followed had significant effects on politics in Iceland. These were exemplified by protests organized (by the normally docile Icelanders) in front of parliament, the resignation of a minister (a highly unusual event in Iceland − see Kristinsson (2008)), and a call for an early election in which the Independence Party lost its status as the biggest party − a position it had maintained since Iceland became independent in 1944. It is also fair to say that the crisis shook the faith of Icelanders in the political system − trust in Althingi dropped from 40% before the crisis to 13%. The political parties received a fair share of distrust as well and came under criticism for not being democratic, engaging in favoritism, and catering to special interests. This distrust of political parties was highlighted by the Best Party's victory in the Reykjavik election in

2010. The Best Party was formed by a comedian – initially as a practical joke – but the party soon found that voters were quite willing to abandon the established parties in favor of a new one. Even if that party made promises such as to make a break with the corrupt practices of the established parties by being openly corrupt. The Best Party secured a plurality of the vote in the election, 34.7%, and the party's leader became the mayor of Reykjavik.

While the crisis has certainly led to events that will qualify as being important in Icelandic political history, what is surprising is that the crisis has not affected the political landscape in a more significant way. Politics has returned to "normal" – any talk of staying united in the face of adversity quickly gave way to parties staking out their positions and, importantly, with MPs toeing the party line with the issue of membership in the EU being the one possible exception. The decision to seek EU membership appeared to be the most significant consequence of the economic crisis – prior to 2009 only one of the major parties had indicated willingness to enter accession negotiations with the EU. However, even this development has returned to "normal" with the IP–PP government withdrawing from the accession negotiations after taking office in 2013.

The early election meant that there was very little time for the dissatisfaction with the political parties to congeal in the form of new political forces capable of challenging the existing parties. The short amount of time provided new political entrepreneurs with limited opportunity to mobilize and build the organizational structures required to run for office. While the decision to call an early election was likely not motivated by concerns of the existing political elite to preserve their positions it appears likely that by doing so it ensured the parties', and its representatives', survival. This is not to say that the 2009 election did not result in an unusually high turnover of MPs. It did, but it was in substantial part due to the swing in the support of the parties rather than significant renewal within the ranks of the parties.

It is clear that the economic crisis shaped the outcome of the 2009 election, e.g., voters sought to hold those responsible for the crisis to account, expressed their dissatisfaction with the political system, and EU membership become a salient election issue at long last. But did the economic crisis have more long-lasting consequences. The early election of 2009 had largely shielded the existing parties from new challengers but new political forces had more time to organize ahead of the April 2013 election. The Civic Movement, the only successful protest party in the 2009 election, disintegrated, to be replaced by a number of smaller parties vying for representation in Althingi. The parties campaigned on issues such as debt relief for mortgage holders, a revival of the failed constitutional reform, and greater transparency. As a result the combined vote share of the four main parties in the 2013 election was only 75% and has rarely been smaller – the average vote share of the four biggest parties from 1963–2009 was 91%. Yet the impact of the new parties was limited thanks to the parties' inability to coordinate their actions in the face of a 5% electoral threshold. Nearly 12% of the vote was wasted on parties that failed to cross the threshold. Only two of the new parties, Bright Future and the Pirate Party, won representation with, respectively, 8.2% and 5.1% of the vote. The Progressive Party having campaigned heavily on mortgage relief made an impressive comeback in the election with 24.4% of the vote – up from 14.8% in the 2009 election. Overall the election could be seen as a marked shift to the right with the Independence Party and the Progressive Party gaining 12.6 percentage points from the previous election. However, it can also be seen as a marked shift away from the government parties, who together lost an impressive 27.7 percentage points between elections. It is somewhat ironic that the influx of new parties – most of which belong to the left side of the political spectrum – paved the way for the formation of a center-right coalition between the Progressive Party and the Independence Party. Although the 2013 election was unusual for the number of parties that contested it and the large shifts in the parties' support, it is not clear yet that the election represents a departure from politics as normal in Iceland. The four biggest parties remain the same and neither of the new parties in Althingi appears likely to pose a serious challenge the status quo. As a protest party, the Pirate Party has a long way to go before being considered "coalitionable" – if at all interested in achieving that status – and will, therefore, remain on the fringes without much influence. Bright Future appears to have better prospects having positioned itself on the center-left as a more pragmatic alternative. Its presence may, however, just be another chapter in the story of the fractured left in Iceland rather than a break with the past.

The Icelandic case is an interesting one in a comparative context. Unlike in many of the countries that have been weathering serious economic crisis, the crisis in Iceland occurred with a right government at the reins. The fact that left and center-left governments in other countries have suffered at the polls means that it is tempting to draw the conclusion that at in times of crisis voters turn to parties on the right as they are seen as more competent in managing the economy or, perhaps, because leftist governments are an easy target of criticism because of their preference for government spending. The Icelandic case suggests that the issue has more to do with incumbency, or accountability, than ideology, which is in line with Bartels's (2012) finding that retrospective voting plays an important role even in times of economic crisis. In Iceland, the government in office when the economy crashed was composed of a right party and center-left party. Rather than abandoning the center-left party, the voters abandoned the right party in droves while the center-left party posted a moderate gain from the previous election. Thus, voters appear to have been more concerned about holding the party responsible accountable for its performance – in this case that was the right party, as the Independence Party had been in office since 1991. Thus, while we can, of course, not tell whether things would have developed differently had the situation been reversed, it suggests, at minimum, that incumbency is an important part of the question.

Notes

1. In combination the three banks constituted about 85% of Iceland's banking system (Gylfason, 2012).
2. The parties represented in Althingi were: The Independence Party (conservative), the Progressive Party (center-right, former farmer's party), The Social Democratic Alliance (center-left), the Left Movement – Greens, and the Liberal Party (center-right).

3. Alternatively, greater concern with unemployment may cause voters to lean left (Kwon, 2008, 2010).

4. The data on expected household income, consumer confidence, and support for government come from Capacent's monthly surveys and are available from http://datamarket.comDatamarket.com.

5. We define government coalitions solely in terms of their party composition. The first coalition according to our definition, the coalition of the Independence Party and the Progressive Party, would normally to be considered as a series of coalitions. The coalition was first led by Davíd Oddsson (IP) who handed the reins of power to Halldór Ásgrímsson (PP) in September 2004 as a part of the parties' agreement to renew their agreement to govern together after the 2003 parliamentary election. Finally, Geir H. Haarde (IP) took over as the Prime Minister on June 15, 2006.

6. The coalition of the Social Democrats and the Left-Green Movement was renewed after a parliamentary election on April 25, 2009, now as a majority coalition, on May 10, 2009.

7. The results of tests for non-stationarity depended on whether the whole time-series was considered or if it was broken down by government. The first two models use *Government Support* as the dependent variable and include lags of *Government Support* to account for autocorrelation. In the next four columns the data are first differenced, i.e., Δ *Government Support* is modeled as a function of change in the independent variables.

8. The questions address current economic and labor market conditions and expectations about economic conditions, labor market conditions, and household income in six months. It bears noting that measures of consumer confidence may be endogenous to the political context (De Boef & Kellstedt, 2004).

9. The effect is statistically significant if the squared value of *Expected Income* is also included in the model.

10. As many, for example Evans & Andersen (2006), Johnston et al. (2005), Wilcox & Wlezien (1993), and Wlezien et al. (1997), have shown there are reasons to believe that partisanship colors evaluations of government performance rather than the other way around. The data used here are evaluations of government performance but the same concerns apply and, thus, the interpretation of the results regarding government performance should be taken with a grain of salt.

11. The models for different years are not fully comparable as some questions were not included in all the surveys. That is obviously the case for questions related to the economic crisis but that was also true about some of the other variables, e.g., *Best Party for Economy*.

12. The effect is calculated by varying the value of each independent variable from its mean $-\frac{1}{2}$ standard deviation to mean $+\frac{1}{2}$ standard deviation while holding other variables fixed at their means except for dichotomous variables, which are held fixed at their mode. The effects of the party-specific variable are not summarized here in a similar manner, as the values of these variables are not independent across parties, i.e., only one party can be considered the best party for the economy. Thus, the effect of being considered the best party for the economy for, say, the SDA depends on which party is initially assumed to be the best party for the economy.

13. Replacing the variable with one based on a question about managing economic recovery yields substantively similar results.

14. The exception is that the effect of *IP-SDA Performance* was positive for the PP ($+6.8\%$ pts) and the respondents were less likely to vote for the SDA (-10.0% pts). It is possible that the respondents that rated the performance of the IP–SDA coalition more highly were also more likely to consider the responsibility for the crisis to lie with non-political actors, i.e., the banks and the FSA, and were less likely to hold the political parties accountable for the crisis. These voters may, therefore, also be less likely to hold the Progressive Party accountable, despite the fact that it had been in government from 1999 to 2007, and support it.

15. The average rating for the IP–PP government in 2007 was 1.69 whereas its successor, the IP–SDA cabinet, had an average rating of 0.79.

16. Following the 2013 election, the government of the IP and the PP halted the accession negotiations.

17. Note that the effects are estimated by holding the values of responsibility at their mean for the other parties but typically holding one party more responsible means holding some other party less responsible. Thus, the estimated effect is likely underestimated.

18. In 2009 the number of respondents that reported a vote for the LP or the CM was relatively small while many respondents had a hard time placing those parties on the left–right policy dimension. The results are very similar when the analysis is restricted to the four main parties.

References

Anderson, C. J. (2000) Economic voting and political context: a comparative perspective. *Electoral Studies*, 19(2–3), pp. 151–170.

Bartels, L. M. (2011) Ideology and retrospection in electoral responses to the great recession. Manuscript.

Bartels, L. M. (2012) Elections in hard times. *Public Policy Research*, 19(1), pp. 44–50.

Capacent (2011) Vidhorf almennings til ESB. Technical report, Samtök idnadarins.

De Boef, S. & Kellstedt, P. M. (2004) The political (and economic) origins of consumer confidence. *American Journal of Political Science*, 48(4), pp. 633–649.

Duch, R. M. & Stevenson, R. T. (2008) *The Economic Vote: How Political and Economic Institutions Condition Election Results*. (Cambridge: Cambridge University Press).

Evans, G. & Andersen, R. (2006) The political conditioning of economic perceptions. *Journal of Politics*, 68(1), pp. 194–207.

Gylfason, T. (2012) From collapse to constitution. CESifo Working Paper No. 3770.

Hardarson, Ó. T. & Kristinsson, G. H. (2010) Iceland. *European Journal of Political Research*, 49(7-8), pp. 1009–1016.

Hellwig, T. (2008). Globalization, policy constraints, and vote choice. *The Journal of Politics*, 70(4), pp. 1128–1141.

Hobolt, S. B. & Tilley, J. (forthcoming) Who's in charge? How voters attribute responsibility in the European Union. *Comparative Political Studies*.

Johnston, R., Sarker, R., Jones, K., Bolster, A., Propper, C., & Burgess, S. (2005) Egocentric economic voting and changes in party choice: Great Britain 1992–2001. *Journal of Elections, Public Opinion & Parties*, 15(1), 129–144.

Key, V. O. (1966) *The Responsible Electorate* (New York: Vintage Books).

Kristinsson, G. H. (2008) More safe than sound: Cabinet ministers in Iceland, in: K. Dowding & P. Dumont (eds) *The Selection of Ministers in Europe: Hiring and Firing* (New York: Routledge).

Kwon, H. Y. (2008) A dynamic analysis of partisan voting: The issue salience effect of unemployment in south korea. *Electoral Studies*, 27(3), pp. 518–532.

Kwon, H. Y. (2010). Unemployment, partisan issue ownership, and vote switching evidence from south korea. *Party Politics*, 1(4), pp. 497–521.

Powell, G. B. & Whitten, G. D. (1993) A cross-national analysis of economic voting: taking account of the political context. *American Journal of Political Science*, 37(2), pp. 391–414.

Strøm, K. (1984) Minority governments in parliamentary democracies: The rationality of nonwinning cabinet solutions. *Comparative Political Studies*, 17(2), pp. 199–227.

Wilcox, N. & Wlezien, C. (1993) The contamination of responses to survey items: Economic perceptions and political judgments. *Political Analysis*, 5(1), pp. 181–213.

Wlezien, C., Franklin, M., & Twiggs, D. (1997) Economic perceptions and vote choice: disentangling the endogeneity. 19(1), pp. 7–17.

Appendix

The estimation results of the mixed logit model are reported in Tables 3–5.[18] The coefficients for the respondent specific variables in Table 3 represent the effects relative to the SDA, e.g., the coefficient for the IP in *Reykjavik* (-1.34^*) indicates that respondents in Reykjavik were less likely to vote for the IP than the SDA and that the difference is statistically significant at the 90% level. The effect for the LM is

Table 3. Vote for party in 2009: mixed conditional logit – Baseline: Social Democratic Alliance

	Alternative Specific Variables				
Left-Right Distance			-0.32^{***}		
			(0.064)		
Responsible for Crisis			-0.12^{**}		
			(0.060)		
Best Party for Economy			1.46^{***}		
			(0.20)		
Party Identifier			2.63^{***}		
			(0.35)		
			Baseline: SDA		
	PP	IP	LM	LP	CM
Reykjavik	-0.56	-1.34*	-0.79*	-0.063	-0.041
	(0.55)	(0.69)	(0.47)	(1.24)	(0.52)
Age	0.0079	0.031	-0.020	-0.019	-0.024
	(0.018)	(0.024)	(0.016)	(0.040)	(0.020)
Female	-1.02^{*}	0.33	0.12	-0.64	-0.75
	(0.57)	(0.67)	(0.47)	(1.15)	(0.56)
Education	-0.013	-0.081	0.073	-0.41	0.23
	(0.14)	(0.16)	(0.13)	(0.30)	(0.15)
Economy 1st or 2nd	-0.52	-0.60	-1.05**	-1.86	-0.22
	(0.50)	(0.64)	(0.46)	(1.24)	(0.51)
IP-SDA Performance	0.74*	1.05**	0.24	0.85	0.069
	(0.39)	(0.47)	(0.35)	(0.83)	(0.38)
SDA-LM Performance	-1.01^{**}	-1.12**	0.64*	-0.36	-0.41
	(0.40)	(0.46)	(0.33)	(0.84)	(0.36)
Pro EU Membership	-0.37^{**}	-0.70***	-0.77***	-0.60	-0.55***
	(0.18)	(0.22)	(0.17)	(0.36)	(0.18)
Political Efficacy	0.0033	0.27*	0.24**	0.52*	-0.085
	(0.12)	(0.16)	(0.12)	(0.29)	(0.12)
Satisfaction w/Democracy	0.13	0.19	-0.17	-0.44	-0.81**
	(0.32)	(0.39)	(0.30)	(0.74)	(0.35)
Institutional Responsibility	-0.22^{***}	-0.22**	-0.12	-0.22*	-0.16**
	(0.079)	(0.087)	(0.077)	(0.13)	(0.079)
Banking Protest	-1.02	-1.27	0.63	-13.2	0.49
	(0.78)	(1.05)	(0.53)	(492.9)	(0.56)
Income Equality	-0.097	0.19	-0.37*	-0.15	-0.33
	(0.20)	(0.22)	(0.21)	(0.44)	(0.21)
Constant	8.53***	3.94	3.47	5.95	7.51***
	(2.85)	(3.37)	(2.76)	(5.57)	(2.85)
N			2790		
Log Likelihood			-269.8		
No. Respondents			465		

* $p < 0.10$, ** $p < 0.05$, *** $p < 0.01$
Standard errors in parentheses

33

Table 4. Vote for party in 2007: mixed conditional logit – Baseline: Social Democratic Alliance

	Alternative Specific Variables				
Left-Right Distance			−0.34***		
			(0.070)		
Environment Policy Distance			−0.31***		
			(0.070)		
Best Party for Tax Policy			0.69***		
			(0.23)		
Party Closest			3.04***		
			(0.20)		
			Baseline: SDA		
	PP	IP	LM	LP	CM
Age	−0.0061	0.015	−0.052***	−0.017	−0.017
	(0.018)	(0.016)	(0.017)	(0.023)	(0.025)
Female	0.23	0.89*	0.031	−1.16	0.53
	(0.55)	(0.48)	(0.48)	(0.78)	(0.71)
Education	−0.084	0.10	−0.042	−0.10	−0.16
	(0.14)	(0.12)	(0.12)	(0.18)	(0.17)
Economy 1st or 2nd	−0.34	−0.12	−0.046	−0.55	0.012
	(0.69)	(0.52)	(0.65)	(0.91)	(0.83)
Gov't Performance	1.21**	0.97**	0.41	−0.43	0.20
	(0.49)	(0.46)	(0.39)	(0.49)	(0.56)
Pro EU Membership	−0.064	−0.063	−0.23	−0.23	−0.25
	(0.20)	(0.17)	(0.19)	(0.24)	(0.26)
Political Efficacy	0.26*	0.21	0.13	0.33*	−0.042
	(0.15)	(0.13)	(0.14)	(0.18)	(0.16)
Satisfaction w/Democracy	0.27	0.58	−0.20	−0.47	−1.05**
	(0.46)	(0.38)	(0.39)	(0.47)	(0.53)
Income Equality	0.078	0.14	−0.29	0.011	0.054
	(0.21)	(0.17)	(0.22)	(0.29)	(0.28)
Reykjavik	−1.16*	−0.16	−0.14	−0.31	0.51
	(0.63)	(0.46)	(0.50)	(0.76)	(0.69)
Constant	−4.21*	−6.35***	2.15	−0.31	2.05
	(2.18)	(1.92)	(1.87)	(2.50)	(2.39)
N			3882		
Log Likelihood			−280.3		
No. Respondents			647		

* $p < 0.10$, ** $p < 0.05$, *** $p < 0.01$
Standard errors in parentheses

also statistically significant from the SDA but the table doesn't show whether the effects for the IP and the LM are statistically different.

The models control for age, gender, education, and preference for income equality. *Education* has seven categories, ranging from respondent not having completed primary education to having an undergraduate degree. The variable *Income Equality*

Table 5. Vote for party in 2003: mixed conditional logit – Baseline: Social Democratic Alliance

	Alternative Specific Variables			
Left-Right Distance		−0.57***		
		(0.061)		
Party Supporter		4.15***		
		(0.40)		
		Baseline: SDA		
	PP	IP	LM	LP
Age	−0.0026	0.0011	−0.012	0.0024
	(0.011)	(0.0073)	(0.014)	(0.0094)
Female	−0.65*	−0.53	−0.37	−0.44
	(0.38)	(0.41)	(0.46)	(0.40)
Education	0.031	0.22**	0.038	0.14
	(0.10)	(0.11)	(0.12)	(0.11)
Economy 1st or 2nd	0.50	1.09**	−0.64	−0.25
	(0.51)	(0.51)	(0.77)	(0.62)
Gov't Performance	1.84***	1.83***	0.84**	0.19
	(0.42)	(0.47)	(0.42)	(0.36)
Pro EU Membership	−0.57***	−0.64***	−0.88***	−0.50***
	(0.15)	(0.16)	(0.19)	(0.16)
Political Efficacy	−0.33**	−0.64***	−0.037	0.13
	(0.17)	(0.18)	(0.21)	(0.16)
Satisfaction w/Democracy	0.25	0.39	−0.51	−0.46*
	(0.28)	(0.30)	(0.31)	(0.27)
Income Equality	−0.073	0.30	−0.88**	0.0031
	(0.20)	(0.20)	(0.37)	(0.21)
Reykjavik	−1.45***	−0.70*	−0.50	−0.72*
	(0.42)	(0.42)	(0.48)	(0.43)
Constant	0.045	0.071	2.76	−0.62
	(1.58)	(1.66)	(1.86)	(1.52)
N		3165		
Log Likelihood		−359.5		
No. Respondents		633		

* $p < 0.10$, ** $p < 0.05$, *** $p < 0.01$
Standard errors in parentheses

is the respondent's answer to the question of whether the state has a role in increasing income equality. Responses to the question are coded on a five-point scale with the lower end of the scale indicating stronger preference for the state's role in promoting income equality.

A Conservative Revolution: The Electoral Response to Economic Crisis in Ireland

MICHAEL MARSH* & SLAVA MIKHAYLOV**

*Department of Political Science, Trinity College Dublin, Ireland; **Department of Political Science, University College London, London

ABSTRACT   *The 2011 election in Ireland was one of the most dramatic elections in European post-war history in terms of net electoral volatility. In some respects the election overturned the traditional party system. Yet it was a conservative revolution, one in which the main players remained the same, and the switch in the major government party was merely one in which one centre-right party replaced another. Comparing voting behaviour over the last three elections we show that the 2011 election looks much like that of 2002 and 2007. The crisis did not result in the redefinition of the electoral landscape. While we find clear evidence of economic voting at the 2011 election, issue voting remained weak. We believe that this is due to the fact that parties have not offered clear policy alternatives to the electorate in the recent past and did not do so in 2011.*

Introduction

The announcement of a "bailout" for the Irish state by the IMF/EU/ECB in November 2010 marked a critical point in the fortunes of the Irish economy and the state's fiscal problems which had been signalled to be in crisis two years earlier when the government felt it necessary to provide a blanket support to the Irish banks. Cuts had been made in many programmes and the pay of public sector workers had been reduced by an average of about 20%. Unemployment soared, from 4.5% at the time of the 2007 election to 14.5% in early 2011. Even as the Dáil (lower house of parliament) approved the terms of the loan, under which stern targets with relation to taxation and spending were set and public policy would be monitored closely until the money was repaid, the government was disintegrating and an election followed soon in February 2011. The result was certainly dramatic: the major party of government and dominant force in the party system, Fianna Fáil (FF), was relegated to third place; the minor partner, the Green Party, lost all its seats; and Fine Gael (FG) became the largest party for the first time and formed a government with the Labour Party, which had almost doubled its vote. Measured in terms of net electoral volatility (the Pedersen index) this was one of the most dramatic elections in European post-war history, and it provided the biggest turnaround in party fortunes that had been seen without the intervention of a significant new party (Mair, 2011). Yet it was arguably a conservative revolution, one in which the main players remained the same, and the switch in the major government party was merely one where one centre-right party replaced another.

This can easily be interpreted as a classic case of economic voting, in which voters punished those responsible for the obvious decline in their collective fortunes, with the added element of public anger at the degree of mismanagement that had taken place (Key, 1966; Powell & Whitten, 1993). We could also see it as further evidence that Ireland fits well into the modern characterization of political competition as "valence" politics (Clarke et al., 2009; Marsh et al., 2008; Stokes, 1963), centred on the economy. This argues that voters will choose the parties seen as most competent to deal with the main – typically economic – issues, and the voters had lost faith in FF as the crisis unfolded. Indeed, poll evidence shows FF support declining sharply as successive stages of the crisis seemed to demonstrate the ineptitude of the government before the more objective indicators were there to confirm economic decline (Marsh & Mikhaylov, 2012). Support went to the obvious alternative, FG and Labour, who had provided the (only) alternative government several times since 1948 but were untainted by responsibility, having been in opposition since 1997.

Yet there were expectations in some quarters, and these have echoes internationally, that the crisis might provide a change in the bases of electoral decision-making. This occasion could have been one in which "policy" choices – and by that we mean choices about how to deal with the crisis – could have been more prominent than they were in recent elections, when the issues around economic management were apparently less urgent and less discussed. The crisis arguably exposed the neo-liberal model of economic management, one that was followed by governments of both centre-left and centre-right across Europe for decades, as having fundamental weaknesses. In consequence there might have been some clear shift away from its tenets and at least a break-up of that consensus. Different groups might define the crisis in different ways – perhaps as a fiscal problem, or by highlighting unemployment – and they may also have different solutions, such as raising taxes on the rich, or cutting expenditure on social welfare. This could have encouraged a sharper left–right divide. Certainly parties of the "left" did unprecedentedly well, winning arguably 31% of the vote,[1] but whether this signified that voters were making an explicit choice of a policy alternative, rather than simply running to anyone but FF, is far less obvious.

While crises such as the Irish one might shake people and institutions out of traditional, almost habitual patterns of behaviour, it is important to acknowledge that such patterns may also be hard to dislodge. There are at least a couple of features of Irish politics that might constrain change. One is the "personal vote", the following that candidates have which may be independent of party; more generally, this includes the importance of candidate relative to party (Carty, 1983; Komito &

Gallagher, 2010; Marsh, 2007). While the appeal of particular candidates obviously did not save Fianna Fáil from an electoral drubbing, it may still be the case that voters' concerns to pick a candidate may inhibit a more ideological politics (e.g. Sacks, 1976). A second is the behaviour of the parties. Arguably, for voters to change, parties have to lead the way. In the past, parties have generally obscured rather than highlighted ideological differences. We will explore the extent to which this was different in 2011.

These are the primary features of the election that will be explored in this article. We will start by looking at the vote in terms of punishment and reward, and consider the importance of blame attribution. We look at what voters thought about the crisis: who was to blame, and who could do a better job in the future. FF did very badly, but how far can the economic crisis explain the scale of the defeat, and the victory of FG and Labour? We will also consider a broader "valence" model such as that advanced by Clark et al. (2009) in which leader and parties are judged in terms of competence to govern. We will then explore how far voters seemed to see this as an election not simply about replacing the government, but of making a choice about future policy directions, with a cleavage along typical economic left–right lines.

Who was to Blame?

There can be little doubt that voters held the government responsible for the crisis, although that is not to say that blame lay solely with that body. The government claimed that much of the reason for the sharp economic downturn and consequent fiscal crisis was external: the collapse of Lehman Brothers and the consequent turmoil in international markets. Independent inquiries set up by the government, but whose remit did not extend to the period of the bank bailout, certainly identified lax regulation as well systemic failures in the Department of Finance, while criminal charges have now been brought against some of the leaders of one of the banks. The Irish Election Study of 2011[2] sought to establish the distribution of culpability across various actors. Table 1 shows the results.

While "bankers" were almost universally accorded a share of the blame, government bodies and the government itself were also held very culpable by a huge majority of voters, almost 80% seeing the government as "very" or "extremely" responsible, and almost 90% feeling the same way about the public servants who were in charge. In contrast, only 60% blamed the international economic situation to the same degree, while the EU and, even more so, Euro membership was relatively innocent. We normally expect responsibility to be conditioned by partisanship, and indeed there is something of this in this data, but only 1% of all voters absolved the government completely and only 8% saw them as less than even "moderately" responsible. FF voters were *more* likely than others to blame civil servants, and *less* likely to blame FF as strongly as other voters, but generally these attributions are at most weakly related to vote. Partisanship does not explain who voters think is most to blame. The key point about this list is that voters tended to place more

Table 1. Responsibility for the crisis

	Not at all	A little	Moderately	Very	Extremely	
	1	2	3	4	5	Mean
Bankers	1	1	5	15	77	4.7
Department of Finance and Irish Central Bank	2	3	9	28	58	4.3
The Irish government	1	7	14	33	45	4.1
International economic situation	3	11	27	32	27	3.7
The European Union	6	16	34	26	17	3.3
Membership of the euro	15	23	27	19	17	3

Note: In the past few years the economy has been in recession. How responsible, if at all, are each of the following for the poor economic conditions of the past two years? Extremely responsible, very responsible, moderately responsible, a little responsible, not at all responsible.

blame at the feet not of international actors and systems but of domestic actors, who either were, or should have been, better regulated by government.

In previous elections in this century there was a greater difference of opinion among voters when it came to blaming, or crediting, governments, and also more variation in perceptions of the government's economic record. Table 2 shows the voters' judgment of the record, the attribution of credit/blame and also considerations as to whether another government might have done better.

The FF-led government was re-elected in 2002 and 2007 (after which the Greens were added to the coalition) with most people seeing the economy as improving, majorities seeing the government as responsible and relatively few thinking the alternative would have done better. This is not surprising: growth was rapid for much of the period, and unemployment had fallen to an unprecedentedly low level, while employment had soared. In 2011, in contrast, with growth stalled, employment falling and unemployment rising rapidly, almost everyone thought the economy had deteriorated considerably, almost everyone blamed the government and this time a sizable minority thought FG and Labour would have done a better job.

A simple multinomial logit model regressing vote on just the variables displayed in Table 2, with added controls for party identification, performs almost equally well in all three years, with pseudo R^2 0.20, 0.20 and 0.17 respectively.[3] Table 3 shows the marginal effects[4] for each of the four main parties in 2011.[5] The model works best, as one might expect, in differentiating FF, the dominant government party. All variables are highly significant in 2011, with the economy also having its strongest effect in that year. The economy does less well in differentiating between the opposition parties. The key factor seems to be whether FG/Labour would have done better: those who thought so were more likely to vote FG and to a lesser extent Labour, while those who did not opted for SF. Those more reluctant to give the government

Table 2. Elements of economic voting

	2002	2007	2011
Economy:			
Got a lot worse	3	3	78
Got a little worse	7	9	16
Stayed the same	10	18	4
Got a little better	40	42	2
Got a lot better	40	28	*
Credit/Blame			
Mainly due to policies of the government	64	66	82
Alternative			
Better	19	11	42
Same	81	62	29
Worse		27	29

Note: Thinking back over the last four years – the lifetime of the 2007 to 2011 Fianna Fáil/PD/ Green government – would you say that the ECONOMY in Ireland over that period of time got a lot better; a little better; stayed the same; got a little worse; or got a lot worse? Do you think this was MAINLY due to the policies of that government or NOT MAINLY DUE to the policies of that government? Would a Fine Gael/Labour coalition have handled the economy better in the past? [This is the 2011 formulation. 2007 and 2002 are different only in terms of lifetime and government composition, except for the 2002 variation below.]
In 2002 the final question was: would any other party have performed better? This is coded here just for FG and/or Labour.
* Less than 0.5%.

credit in 2002 and 2007 also are more likely to vote FG. If we model the choice as simply that between FF and FG, pseudo R^2 rises to 0.32, 0.28 and 0.32 across 2002–2011, with all effects highly significant in 2011 and the credit/blame effect particularly marked, adding 17% to the FG share of the combined FG/FF vote.[6]

All this suggests that the economic voting model helps to tell us why FF did so badly in 2011. Times were bad, and there is evidence that voters blamed FF more when times were bad than they credited the party when times were good. The model also helps to account for why FG and to a lesser extent Labour capitalized, but not why voters chose one of them rather than the other, and it is even less successful at explaining the change elsewhere in the system, nor why the huge number of voters who deserted FF ended up where they did.[7]

It has been argued that assessments of leaders play a critical role in voters' electoral choice, although many argue that the effects, while they may be critical in a close election, are relatively small in the context of a party's overall vote. It is of course problematic to separate leader and party evaluations, since each may be contaminated by the other (see Clarke et al., 2009; Curtice & Holmerg, 2005; Miller & Shanks, 1996). Keeping this in mind we explored the added value of leader evaluations for the models run above. The question items used here all asked voters to say how

Table 3. Average marginal effects of economic vote model with party attachment (standard errors in brackets)

		2002	2007	2011
Fianna Fail	Economy	-0.030*	-0.024	-0.059***
		(0.017)	(0.021)	(0.020)
	Responsibility	0.129***	0.120***	-0.131***
		(0.021)	(0.028)	(0.026)
	Alternative	-0.240***	-0.216***	-0.072***
		(0.028)	(0.042)	(0.017)
Fine Gael	Economy	0.009	0.012	0.048
		(0.014)	(0.019)	(0.047)
	Responsibility	-0.040**	-0.052*	0.051
		(0.019)	(0.027)	(0.033)
	Alternative	0.190***	0.108**	0.136***
		(0.03)	(0.046)	(0.025)
Labour	Economy	0.016*	0.004	-0.053
		(0.009)	(0.014)	(0.032)
	Responsibility	-0.021	-0.002	0.048*
		(0.013)	(0.02)	(0.025)
	Alternative	0.085***	0.104***	0.034*
		(0.021)	(0.039)	(0.020)
Sinn Fein	Economy	0.011*	0.012	-0.003
		(0.007)	(0.009)	(0.027)
	Responsibility	-0.006	-0.026*	0.005
		(0.010)	(0.014)	(0.019)
	Alternative	-0.018*	-0.022	-0.041***
		(0.011)	(0.017)	(0.014)
Log Likelihood		-1947	-1096	-1926
Pseudo R^2		0.199	0.197	0.167
Pseudo R^2: party attachment only		0.165	0.177	0.139
Observations		1,767	983	1,578

Note: Standard errors in parentheses. *** $p<0.01$, ** $p<0.05$, * $p<0.10$. Effects of party attachment and effect on Others not shown.

good a leader was at "running the country", using a 0–10 scale. This was asked of four party leaders in 2011, those of FG, FF, Labour and SF, but only of a subset of these in previous studies. The FG leader was rated more highly than the FF leader only in 2011, but even then his lead was much smaller than the FF lead in 2002 and 2007.

If we add these leader variables to the first regression model discussed earlier, explained variance for 2011, using all four leaders, rises from 0.17 (see Table 3) to 0.28.[8] Adding just the FF and FG leaders, it also improves in each of the three years. The leaders' marginal effects are generally all significant, adding up to 6% (in the case of Labour in 2011) to a party's vote. The main point here, however, is not whether leaders mattered, or how much they mattered, but to show that even using a more inclusive understanding of valence politics (on the economy) containing parties and leaders, the 2011 election looks much like that of 2002 and 2007. The models are really no more, or less, effective in explaining voting in 2011 than they are in previous years. FF lost because it and its leaders were seen to have done a very poor job, and FG and Labour were a better bet for the future, the converse of 2002 and 2007.

Evidence for Issue-Based Voting

So far the evidence suggests that valence politics, at least with respect to the economy, were no less important in 2011 than in previous years. We now move on to look at whether or not judgments about competence were supplemented by concerns about the direction of policy, most notably in relation to the economy, but also the substitution of non-economic issues for economic ones. On this second point the salient issue of the 2011 election as measured directly by surveys was the economy, but within that fairly broad concern voters did emphasize different aspects of the overall problem. Asked to name the two most important issues to them personally, 58% mentioned some aspect of the crisis, and 54% a more specific economic issue. Whilst 26% highlighted the fact that the government or the system had let them down, another 26% mentioned another (essentially non-economic) issue, the most frequently cited being the health system. Overall, a massive 86% of voters mentioned either the crisis or an economic issue. With respect to particular economic issues, most (43%) highlighted job creation. Perhaps this might plausibly be seen as indicating a concern for the policies of growth over those of austerity. Just over 50% of Labour and SF supporters talked about jobs, as against 40% of FF voters and just 37% of FG voters. More generally, however, the issues mentioned by each voter generally relate weakly, if at all, to electoral choice, and even job creation explains less than 1% of the variance in vote choice. All parties' manifestos recognized job creation as necessary, but there is also some evidence from opinion polls during the campaign that Labour outperformed FG on the jobs issue, while on the deficit and the banking issue FG was most capable (Marsh & Cunningham, 2011: 188–189). Dealing with the crisis required policies to fill the hole in the public finances. Job creation, all agreed, was one part of that, although the parties on the left, like the trade unions, saw a stronger role for government in achieving it.

More generally, the choice was one of increasing state income and/or reducing expenditure, the tax/spend trade-off that typically separates left and right. The terms of the IMF/EU/ECB deal were set by the time of the election, and only SF – perhaps knowing it would be in opposition anyway – promised to tear up the agreement. There were differences between parties over the time scale for eliminating the deficit with trade unions and SF setting a longer time horizon. FG and Labour (and SF) differed on the balance of tax increases and expenditure cuts, with SF arguing for more taxes on the most well off, FG resisting almost any increase in direct taxation and Labour looking to cut the deficit using tax increases and spending cuts equally (Suiter & Farrell, 2011: 36–38).

Two questions were asked in the election study about this trade-off. One was the conventional increase tax/cut spending item and the other, in the spirit of the times, counterposed tax increases and small cuts with no tax increases and larger cuts.[9] Both items employed a 0–10 scale. The distribution of responses was almost identical, with a fairly even balance around a high peak at 5, although the correlation between the two sets of responses was only a little over 0.5.

Figure 1 shows the changing distribution of responses to a conventional question on this trade-off. There is a leftward bias to the distribution in 2011, but this is actually less pronounced than in previous years. In particular, very few placed themselves on the extreme left point; 2011 saw a marked increase in placing themselves at the sixth and seventh point. In 2007, with all parties offering to reduce taxation (still further), there was arguably less attention given to this trade-off, and more attention to areas that required more spending, notably health. Property taxes were providing the state with a comfortable surplus. Nor did the major parties discuss increasing taxes in 2002. The tax cuts in the previous decade were popular; rather Labour and FG each focussed on improving the quality of public services, to be paid for in a painless fashion. We might expect that 2011 would see a significant link between a voter's position on this broad issue, and vote, however weak this might have been earlier.[10]

Using this and several other measures of economic policy preference to model vote suggests only a tenuous link between such preferences and party choice in any of the years covered by the Irish election studies. Marginal effects from a multinomial logit regression, also including partisanship, are shown in Table 4.

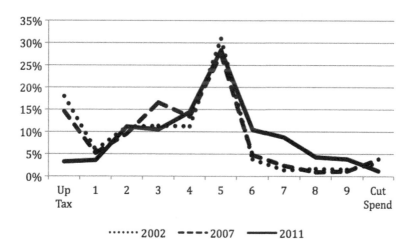

Figure 1. Distribution of tax/spend preferences.
Note: I would like you to look at the scale from 0 to 10 below. A "0" means government should CUT TAXES A LOT and SPEND MUCH LESS on health and social services, and "10" means government should INCREASE TAXES A LOT and SPEND MUCH MORE on health and social services. Where would you place yourself in terms of this scale? This scale has been reversed in the graph here, so that "left" is 0 and "right" is 10.

Table 4. Average marginal effects of policy preference model with party attachment (standard errors in brackets)

		2002	2007	2011	2011
Fianna Fail	Tax/spend	-0.002	0.007	-0.005	
		(0.005)	(0.006)	(0.004)	
	More regulation	0.002	-0.003	-0.005*	-0.006*
		(0.004)	(0.006)	(0.003)	(0.003)
	Ordinary people get fair share [disagree]	0.007	0.017**	0.004	0.006
		(0.006)	(0.008)	(0.005)	(0.005)
	Nothing wrong with some being richer [agree]	0.008	0.013	0.012**	0.014**
		(0.006)	(0.01)	(0.006)	(0.006)
	More private ownership				0.003
					(0.003)
	Tax/spend (2011)				0.002
					(0.004)
Fine Gael	Tax/spend	0.003	0.001	0.003	
		(0.004)	(0.006)	(0.006)	
	More regulation	0.001	-0.000	0.009**	0.009*
		(0.004)	(0.005)	(0.004)	(0.005)
	Ordinary people get fair share [disagree]	-0.000	-0.011	0.011	0.012
		(0.005)	(0.007)	(0.007)	(0.007)
	Nothing wrong with some being richer [agree]	-0.001	-0.011	0.021**	0.024***
		(0.005)	(0.008)	(0.009)	(0.009)
	More private ownership				-0.004
					(0.005)
	Tax/spend (2011)				-0.001
					(0.006)
Labour	Tax/spend	0.003	0.000	0.003	
		(0.003)	(0.004)	(0.005)	
	More regulation	-0.002	-0.004	-0.006*	-0.006
		(0.003)	(0.004)	(0.004)	(0.004)
	Ordinary people get fair share [disagree]	-0.001	0.006	0.005	0.002
		(0.004)	(0.005)	(0.006)	(0.006)
	Nothing wrong with some being richer [agree]	-0.004	0.009	-0.021***	-0.021***
		(0.004)	(0.007)	(0.007)	(0.007)
	More private ownership				-0.001
					(0.004)
	Tax/spend (2011)				0.004
					(0.005)

(*Continued*)

44

Table 4. (*Continued*)

		2002	2007	2011	2011
Sinn Fein	Tax/spend	0.000	-0.004	-0.007**	
		(0.002)	(0.003)	(0.003)	
	More regulation	0.001	-0.001	0.002	0.003
		(0.002)	(0.002)	(0.003)	(0.003)
	Ordinary people get fair share [disagree]	-0.002	-0.013***	-0.007	-0.008*
		(0.003)	(0.005)	(0.004)	(0.004)
	Nothing wrong with some being richer [agree]	0.002	-0.008**	-0.008	-0.013**
		(0.003)	(0.004)	(0.005)	(0.005)
	More private ownership				-0.001
					(0.003)
	Tax/spend (2011)				-0.005
					(0.003)
Log Likelihood		-1931	-1084	-1662	-1639
Pseudo R^2		0.163	0.181	0.158	0.153
Pseudo R^2: party attachment only		0.161	0.167	0.146	0.14
Observations		1,670	955	1,351	1,326

Note: Standard errors in parentheses. *** $p<0.01$, ** $p<0.05$, * $p<0.10$.

Two points are very clear. The first is that these have a weak relationship with vote choice. The second is that this applies in 2011 as it did in 2002: there is no evidence of a closer link in 2011 despite the crisis and salience of the underlying issues. We would expect to see largely positive marginal effects for the centre-right parties, FF and FG, and negative ones for the centre-left and left parties, Labour and SF. Marginal effects are all small, even allowing for the fact that these are 11- and 7-point scales. The tax/spend issue has little significance, with only SF in 2011 showing a marginal effect at 0.05, and in the expected, negative direction (favouring higher taxes). Regulation seems more important in 2011: again, this has the unexpected sign for FF, and is not significant for SF. The public/private ownership item, available only in 2011, has no significant marginal effects. Finally, only one of the two measures capturing attitudes to equality has any significant effects, with Labour and SF voters (the latter only in the setting with a rephrased 2011 tax/spend question) disagreeing that there is nothing wrong with some being a lot richer than others, while FF and FG voters agree. This item is perhaps the most effective discriminator between the parties of the left and those of the right, but only in 2011. The equality items were previously significant for SF in 2007. Overall then, there is little here to suggest any of those issues that we typically see as providing the substance of left–right debate, at least as measured here, had much impact on voting choice and no sign that they had more effect in 2011.

However, if we move away from such issue questions and look simply at voters' own reported positions on a left–right scale, there does seem to be a much stronger relationship with vote choice. Figure 2 shows changes in the left–right self-placement distribution over time. In 2011 voters seem to have moved slightly to the right, with less than one-third placed on the mid point. Essentially the change is a net shift of about 10% of voters from point 5 to point 6.

More important for our purpose here is how this translated into party choice, particularly as the "left" performed better in 2011 than previously. Adding this assessment to the regression that underlies Table 4 provides evidence to suggest that self-placement is associated very significantly with voting, although there is no consistent evidence of a strengthening effect. It is stronger for FG in 2011 (0.054***, as against 0.008 and 0.011 in 2002 and 2007 respectively) and SF (-0.024*** as against -0.009** and -0.004 in 2002 and 2007) but not for Labour (consistently left), or FF (consistently right).[11] These effects, while generally significant, and always so in 2011, are still pretty modest ones. The left, in broad terms, is more obviously separate from the centre-right parties, but looking at where voters of the different parties are now placed there is little evidence of much of a shift to the left.

Table 5, which shows how voters place both themselves and each party, suggests that the average voter for each of the parties has moved to the right since 2002 and 2007, and even that of SF has remained in the same position as 2007. The shift is particularly striking in the case of FG and Labour. Of course, both parties increased their vote significantly, but an influx of new voters does not explain the change, as those who claimed to have voted for each of those parties in 2007 are now also to the right

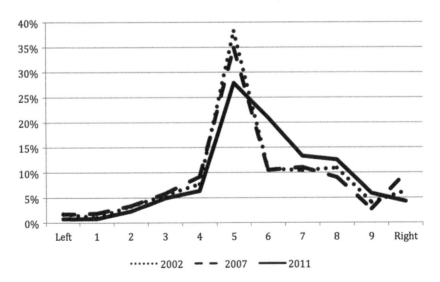

Figure 2. Left–right self-placement.
Note: In politics people sometimes talk of left and right. Where would you place yourself on a scale from 0 to 10 where 0 means the left and 10 means the right?

Table 5. Left–right mean position of parties, 2002–2011

	Self-placement by party's voters			Voters' placement of each party		
	2002	2007	2011	2002	2007	2011
FF	6.4	6.4	6.6	6.4	6.6	6
PD	6.2	6.1	n/a	6.2	6.2	n/a
FG	6	5.8	6.6	6	6.1	6.8
Ind/Other	5.4	5.3	5.5	n/a	n/a	n/a
Labour	4.6	4.6	5.4	3.7	4.1	4.5
Green	4.4	4.4	5.3	4.4	4.4	4.2
SF	4.4	4.6	4.6	3.1	3.5	2.9

of the voters of 2007. There was certainly no shift to the left, nor was there any obvious polarization within the system, and on the economic dimensions the shifts were, if anything, in a rightward direction.

We suggested that the view that voters might choose parties in 2011 based on tax/spend preferences had some plausibility, even if the evidence suggested that this calculus was not something that approximated to the thinking of many voters. The evidence is much better when we see voter ideology in more general terms, and while the signs that left–right voting might be intensifying are flimsy, they are not inconsistent with this view. However, there are anomalies; voters seem to have moved to the right as more of them voted for parties on the left, while those who did support left-wing parties saw them as more right-wing than did supporters in 2002 and 2007!

A further problem is that what voters mean by left and right is, at best, unclear. Voters have traditionally resisted such direct left–right self-placement measures, opting for the middle point (or the apparent middle point on a 10-point scale) or giving no response (Inglehart & Klingemann, 1976; Sinnott, 1995), suggesting that the concept was not familiar to many. In 2011 only about 13% of voters could not place parties on a left–right scale, and slightly more, 16%, were unable to place themselves, which suggests more familiarity with the terms than was the case 40 years ago. More importantly, previous analysis has suggested that the Irish electorate tends not to associate equality with public enterprise and management, two elements of left–right ideology closely linked elsewhere (Kennedy & Sinnott, 2006). Neither of these traditional indicators makes much of a contribution to explaining vote choice. Nor do they predict left–right self-placement very well! A simple test is the regression of self-placement on the tax/spend and regulation items above, plus two items tapping attitudes to inequality.[12] The tax/spend preferences are significantly associated with left–right only in 2007, although the 2011 reformulation is also significant at the even more marginal 0.10 level. Regulation is related consistently to self-placement (apart from 2007), and attitudes to private ownership are not significant at all. The items on inequality are also consistently associated with self-placement. Altogether though, these four indicators explain little variance in voters' positioning; we do not explain more than 4% of the variance.[13] The highest explained variance is achieved in 2007.[14] Of course it is possible that left–right self-placement is not about economic or even equality issues as much as it is about other issues, such as a broadly religious versus a secular view of society. Indeed, when an item asking whether or not God exists is added to the regression it outperforms all other items and more than doubles the variance explained. Party support explains a lot more than economic, or religious, factors, raising the possibility that placement may be better seen as a consequence rather than as a cause of vote choice (see also Marsh et al., 2008).

Parties and Candidates

One factor commonly seen to inhibit issue-based representation is the importance of individual candidates to voters, and the fact that candidate appeal is rooted in parochial activities and concerns. Such attitudes might be a factor in obscuring the sort of relationships we have been exploring here, and that the "clientelist" mode of politics which sustains the importance of candidate is one which inhibits the development of (national) issue-centred politics, particularly around a left–right economic cleavage (e.g. Higgins, 1982; Sacks, 1976). One response to the crisis could have been to direct attention away from merely local concerns and onto national ones. Anecdotal evidence from the campaign "doorsteps" and earlier suggests some change. A senior FG politician explained to one author at the start of the crisis that he was being told by supporters that he belonged in Dublin, sorting out the country, rather than holding "clinics" in his constituency; a senior Labour politician reported that he was being asked during the campaign to discuss solutions to the debt crisis rather than what could be done about local potholes in the road. Would "policy" trump "looking after the constituency" in 2011?

Assessing the weight of candidates and parties in the vote is far from being straightforward, as support for each almost certainly spills over to the other. Parties gain support from running a "good" candidate, but the party label influences the way voters see that candidate. Parties certainly cultivate promising candidates, whether or not they have a long history in the party, and will often nominate those with close family ties to former incumbents, thus combining candidate and party assets. Respondents in the election studies were asked whether party or candidate was most important in their vote. The results show a striking change from 2002–2007 to 2011: from almost 60:40 emphasizing the candidate in 2002–2007, the weightings are almost exactly reversed in 2011. It is also notable that FF voters were now more likely to emphasize the candidate and FG voters less likely to do so. Overall this ties in somewhat with campaign polls, which seemed to show that voters stressed "policy" more than in past years, and – though evidence here is more varied – placed less emphasis on picking a candidate to serve the constituency (Marsh & Cunningham, 2011: 184–186).[15]

However, there is little sign that the more party-centred voter is any more likely to behave ideologically. There are only modest differences between party and candidate-centred voters in model fit.[16] This seems on the face of it a curious result. While questions might be asked of the measure of party-centredness here (but see footnote 15) the fact remains that overall the ideological model fits poorly. One further reason for that could lie in the parties and how they present themselves rather than with concerns of the voters. We have referred in passing to the stances taken by parties in the 2011 election, but we can now look at this more systematically, comparing positions in 2011 to those in earlier years.

We used the data from the Manifesto Project for the elections from 1992 to 2011. Following Lowe et al. (2011) we rescaled the data using the empirical logit transformation that better captures the characteristics of underlying data, dynamic movement of parties on the dimensions of interest over time, and spatial politics assumptions about the range of ideal points (for details see also Benoit et al., 2012). We will look here at just three things: state involvement in economy;[17] state-provided services;[18] and finally, the general left–right dimension.[19] In each case we will show results for the positions of parties and also for the importance of the issue. What we are looking for here is evidence of a change in the "supply side" in 2011, an indication that on economic issues in particular, as well as in broader left–right terms, the electorate was offered a sharper choice in this election than previously, which might have provided the voters with a clearer definition of the differences between the parties. We are also interested in whether there is any substance behind the apparent rightward shift by voters evident in the earlier analysis, particularly around Table 5 and Figure 2.

The dimension of state involvement in the economy captures the balance between market orthodoxy and liberalism on the right and higher involvement of the state in running the economy and supporting the welfare state on the left. Figure 3 (panel A) shows the positions of main parties on this dimension, and the importance of the dimension to the electoral platforms of the parties. The results correspond to conventional understanding of positions of Irish parties on the economic dimension, with FG and FF being pretty close to each other, Labour being further to the left outflanked only by SF. At the 2011 elections there appears to be a reversal of a long-term trend leftward by FF and FG, with the movement to the right by all four parties (albeit Labour started off on that trend already after the 2002 election). The importance of that dimension has grown for FF, FG and Labour since 2002. It also appears that, positionally, three of the four parties are close to one another, and as close in 2011 as at any other time in the period covered. In other words, there was no obvious movement by the parties to provide any sharper definition of left and right in these terms in 2011.

Much the same is true on the state-provided services dimension. Panel B of Figure 3 provides party positions and importance of this dimension for parties. This dimension provides information drawn from the nature of references to welfare state and education limitations as opposed to expansion. Again we see a rightward move in 2011 with the three largest parties as close as at any time since 1992. Only SF provides a contrast. The importance of this issue appears to have declined slightly in 2011, more sharply for FF.

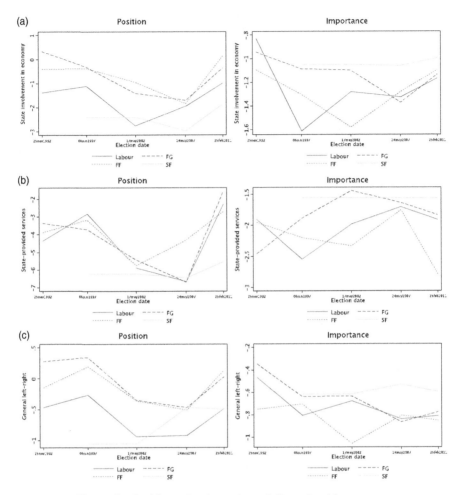

Figure 3. Positions of main parties and dimensional importance.
Note: Manifesto Project data rescaled with the empirical logit transformation following Lowe et al. (2011). Positions of main political parties on three dimensions: State involvement in economy, state-provided services, and general left–right.

Finally, panel C of Figure 3 shows an overall left–right dimension, drawn from 26 categories in the manifesto analysis. Again this shows a rightward shift by all but SF, with again, no obvious broadening of the gap between left and right parties, and FF and FG virtually indistinguishable. There was no change in importance.

Conclusion

This article explores the 2011 election in Ireland, which was fought in the immediate aftermath of a "bailout" made necessary by a major fiscal and banking crisis. In some respects the election overturned the traditional party system. This provides an extreme case of poor economic performance under the incumbent government, made more stark by the fact that the main incumbent party had been in office for 14 years. The central question was how well we can understand the result in these terms, as a classic case of retrospective voting. It appears to be a good illustration of economic voting: when the economy appeared to be in good shape the government was returned, and when it was performing very poorly, and it was very sick indeed in 2011, the government was punished. There is, however, no clear sign in this analysis that it was the variation in economic evaluations in 2011 as such that mattered, perhaps because there was such widespread agreement that matters were critical. More important were the perceptions of accountability and the assessment of the alternative. This approach also does tell us much about the performance of the other parties in the system and why FG seems to capitalize best on FF's collapse. More general models incorporating leaders not surprisingly perform better without telling us quite why the earthquake was so devastating.

We also explored the possibility that the crisis prompted some change from an election driven by the choice of the most competent party, to one driven by a concern for what a party might do, a shift to positional voting away from valence voting. One possibility was that the growth in the vote for parties of the left seen in 2011 was directly attributable to the nature of the crisis, with more people adopting left-wing positions. Indeed, to the extent that the crisis is an indictment of neo-liberal economic management, we might have expected some redefinition of Irish electoral competition. Again, there was little sign of this. The electorate, if anything, seemed to move to the right, and perceived parties – even left-wing ones – as doing so too. We looked at a number of policy choices and preferences, most notably the tax/spend trade-off, but could find no sign that the electorate engaged with parties in these terms. These sorts of issues, or attitudes, had at best a very weak relationship with vote choice in 2011, just as they did in earlier years. A possible exception is that a voter's own location of themselves on a left–right spectrum does relate strongly to vote choice, but it is argued here that the evidence suggests this is a placement that reflects vote as much as it determines it, with placement very weakly linked to issues.

We then considered two reasons why issue voting of this sort was so weak. The first is the importance of candidates rather than parties for many voters, an importance that is arguably linked more closely to the provision of real and imaginary benefits to an area than to a candidate's ideological position. Voters did seem to give more weight to parties this time, claiming that parties (and policy) were more important. However, more party-centred voters appear to be hardly more ideological than their counterparts.

We also looked at the supply side: were the parties offering a clear choice to the voters. The pattern here was generally in accord with voters' self-placements and assessments: parties moved to the right and the distance between them did not change significantly and arguably remained small. If voters did not vote in accordance with their views on taxing and spending, for instance, perhaps this was in part due to their chronic and understandable inability to distinguish what the parties were promising. This is in line with what LeDuc and Pammett (in press) call the "politics of discontent", where governing parties may be replaced without any serious discussion of the crisis (causes and solutions) in the campaign by all parties. They suggest this is partly because parties arrive at an implicit consensus on the direction of economic policy and do not formulate alternative economic policy solutions, but it can also be difficult to present clear alternatives to the voters when this has not been the norm in the past. Mair (1992) argued that the reasons for the weakness of the left in Ireland lay not with the weakness of industrialization – hardly plausible now – not even with "clientelism" – but rather with the unusual ability of FF to attract support across the social spectrum and with the strategy of the Labour Party to opt for a small share in government rather than continued opposition whenever it was offered. This state of affairs has served to sustain valence politics, particularly when the national cleavage that underlay the FF–FG division lost its salience. FF's dominance is unlikely to be repeated, but with a FG/Labour government in place, and FF/SF in opposition, there is little more clarity on offer as yet and the odds are that valence-based voting will predominate over substance-based positional voting for some time to come.

This analysis carried some implications for comparative research. First, while it does provide a good example of economic voting, it shows clearly attribution is the most important element in voters' calculations, and here this helps to show how some voters rationalized their decision to stay with FF or switch to an alternative. In general this alternative was seen as better able to do a good job; those who blamed FF, but were not attracted by the alternative, opted for "third" parties and independents. Second, this case shows little sign that the current crisis has prompted any significant move towards a more policy salient vote. Perhaps there are features of Irish politics that have traditionally discouraged such a focus. If so, these have not changed markedly, and even if voters claim to be more party-centred, those parties did little to identify their own policy responses clearly in the public mind. Of course the lack of change should be seen in the context of the timing of the election as the first one of the economic crisis. It was natural for voters to switch to parties that might be similar, but different: a familiar set of parties, who could not easily be blamed for the disaster. If there is little improvement before the next election, due in 2016, that might prompt a greater change, but even so the absence of a clear left and right element in government–opposition conflict suggests that even though the next election might see a high level of volatility, it will not be driven by stronger positional voting.

Notes

1. This is the combined vote of the centrist left Labour (19.4%), the nationalist left Sinn Fein (SF) (9.9%) and the United Left Alliance (2.7%). If we add the Green Party (1.8%) it would rise to 32.8%. In 2007 these combined parties won only 21.6%, with the Greens contributing 4.6%.
2. This was a post-election study of 1,853 respondents with interviewing completed a few weeks after the election. Households were selected using a random route method starting from 320 locations drawn from all 43 constituencies. Interviewees were chosen within households to fit demographic quotas.

3. We included party identification to allow for the possibility that many voters would view the world through partisan spectacles (Campbell et al., 1960; Duch et al., 2000; see also Evans & Andersen, 2006, for a stronger critique). For a contrary view see Green et al. (2002). Partisanship – measured by the question asking are you close to any political party – is very low, with only about a quarter of voters admitting to such an identification, and dropping to 20% in 2011, as FF partisans vanished. Clearly, this measure cannot be seen as wholly independent of recent experiences. We opted for a simple model without interactions (c.f. Marsh & Tilley, 2010) because including the responsibility measure and the assessment of an alternative ran the risk of overcorrecting for a partisan bias. As we see, the partisanship variables seem to be doing most of the work. Without them the pseudo R^2 is much lower, 0.08, 0.04 and 0.05, respectively.

4. The parameters of multinomial models are not directly interpretable but their significance can be immediately discerned. Much of our discussion below specifically revolves around the analysis of significance of individual coefficients (and overall model performance). However, in multinomial models coefficients can be calculated only in relation to the baseline category (Fine Gael in our case), while we would prefer to have the effects for all parties. This can be achieved by changing the focus from the logit coefficients to the marginal effects that can be calculated for all categories (parties). The marginal effects in multinomial models capture the impact of a change in the predictor on the probability of observing each of several alternative outcomes. The table presents average marginal effects (AMEs) for each of the alternatives with corresponding uncertainty estimates. The reported results are derivatives (or discrete first-differences for factor variables) of the response with respect to the key predictors, i.e. it captures a change in the response for a change in the predictor.

5. All other parties are included with Independents as Others. The numbers voting for each of these are too small to analyse usefully in this manner. Independents are a very disparate group and we have not shown the independents/others effects, but they are generally not significant.

6. Full results from this estimation are not shown here to preserve space. They are available from the authors upon request.

7. A special feature of 2011 that attracted comment was the degree of anger felt by many voters as they were let down by the government and the financial elite, and politicians in general, with large salaries and generous expenses and very comfortable pensions and severance payments. On a scale of 1–5, where 5 is "extremely angry" the median voter was at 4: very angry at "how things were going in the country these days". Including this emotion adds only marginally to the fit of the models run above, but does suggest SF and Independent voters were even angrier than those of FG and Labour.

8. The results are available from the authors upon request.

9. I would like you to look at the scale from 0 to 10 below. A "0" means government should CUT TAXES A LOT and SPEND MUCH LESS on health and social services, and "10" means government should INCREASE TAXES A LOT and SPEND MUCH MORE on health and social services. Where would you place yourself in terms of this scale? This scale has been reversed in the discussion here, so that "left" is 0 and "right" is at 10. In 2011, arguably, the choice was not so much one between increasing tax or cutting spending, but how much tax should increase *and* how far spending should be cut. For this reason the INES asked a second question: I would like you to look at the scale from 0 to 10 on this card. A "0" means government should MAINTAIN TAXES and SPEND LESS on health and social services, and "10" means government should INCREASE TAXES A LOT and SPEND THE SAME on health and social services. Where would you place yourself in terms of this scale? There is very little difference in either the distribution, or the effects on vote between these two wordings.

10. We find much the same picture if we look at another measure designed to tap positions on a left–right scale. There was an increase in support for more rather than less regulation in 2011, for instance, although there was also an increase for private rather than public enterprise.

11. Full results are available from authors upon request.

12. Full results are available from authors upon request.

13. A similar analysis was carried out on the 1990 World Values Study, but with different measures and results that suggested bigger differences between parties than we find here: see Hardiman and Whelan (1994).

14. This was the final wave of a five-wave study, and even though it was supplemented to achieve a more representative sample, it is likely that the voters in 2007 were more sophisticated than those in 2002 or 2011.

15. Such self-reporting may be considered unreliable, and may reflect a perception that parties *should* be more important rather than real motivation. However, there is separate evidence that more voters did give a priority to parties. Those voting a "straight ticket" – giving a preference to all candidates for one party before those of a second party – did rise in 2011. This comes from the mock ballots filled in by election study respondents. (For a discussion of this method see Marsh et al., 2008.) Moreover, those who said they were more party-centred did fill in their ballots in a more party-centred way. *Using the combined measure above, only 34% of candidate-centred voters cast a straight ticket compared with 55% of party-centred voters. Comparable percentages for 2002 and 2007 are 23 and 58, and 27 and 58.*

16. For 2011, Pseudo R^2 is 0.028 and 0.019 for party- and candidate-centred voters respectively using the variables in Table 4, column 3 without party attachment. If a behavioural measure (and the number of cases is necessarily smaller here) it is used, R^2 for those voting a straight party ticket is 0.043 and 0.025 for those who do not.

17. Lowe et al. (2011) define the "right" side of the dimension state involvement in economy as a combination of positive reference to free enterprise, economic incentives, economic orthodoxy, welfare state limitations, and negative references to protectionism. The "left" side is defined by positive references to market regulation, economic planning, protectionism, controlled economy, nationalization, welfare state expansion, education expansion, and labour groups. Position on the dimension is then scaled as the empirical logit transform of the difference between right and left. Thus more negative positions reflect more "leftist" positions.

18. Lowe et al. (2011) define the "right" side of the dimension state-provided services as a combination of positive reference to welfare state limitation, education provision limitation. The "left" side is defined by positive references to welfare state expansion, and education provision expansion. Position on the dimension is then scaled as the empirical logit transform of the difference between right and left. Thus more positive positions reflect more "rightist" positions.

19. General left–right is a combination of 26 categories from manifesto analysis, capturing a variety of left and right issues.

References

Benoit, Kenneth, Laver, Michael, Lowe, Will & Mikhaylov, Slava (2012) How to scale coded text units without bias: a response to Gemenis. *Electoral Studies*, 31(3), pp. 605–608.

Campbell, Angus, Converse, Philip, Miller, Warren & Stokes, Donald E. (1960) *The American Voter* (Chicago: University of Chicago Press).

Carty, Xavier (1983) *Elections '82: What the Papers Said?: An Analysis of Press Coverage of the Two 1982 General Elections in the Republic of Ireland* (Dublin: Able Press).

Clarke, Harold, Sanders, David, Stewart, Marianne C. & Whiteley, Paul F. (2009) *Performance Politics and the British Voter* (Cambridge: Cambridge University Press).

Curtice, J. & Holmerg, S. (2005) Party leaders and party choice, in: J. Thomassen (ed.) *The European Voter* (Oxford: Oxford University Press), pp. 235–253.

Duch, Raymond, Palmer, Harvey & Anderson, Christopher J. (2000) Heterogeneity in perceptions of national economic conditions. *American Journal of Political Science*, 44, pp. 863–881.

Evans, Geoffrey & Andersen, Robert (2006) The political conditioning of economic perceptions: evidence from the 1992–97 British electoral cycle. *Journal of Politics*, 68, pp. 194–207.

Green, Donald, Palmquist, Bradley & Schickler, Eric (2002) *Partisan Hearts and Minds: Political Parties and the Social Identities of Voters* (New Haven: Yale University Press).

Hardiman, Niamh & Whelan, Christopher T. (1994) Values and political partisanship, in: Christopher T. Whelan (ed.) *Values and Social Change in Ireland* (Dublin: Gill and Macmillan), pp. 100–135.

Higgins, Michael D. (1982) The limits of clientelism: towards an assessment of Irish politics, in: Christopher Clapham (ed.) *Private Patronage and Public Power* (London: Frances Pinter), pp. 114–141.

Inglehart, Ronald & Klingemann, Hans-Dieter (1976) Party identification, ideological preference, and the left-right dimension among western mass publics, in: Ian Budge, Ivor Crewe & Dennis Farlie (eds) *Party Identification and Beyond: Representations of Voting and Party Competition* (New York: Wiley), pp. 243–273.

Kennedy, Fiachra & Sinnott, Richard (2006) Irish social and political cleavage, in: John Garry, Niamh Hardiman & Diane Payne (eds) *Irish Social and Political Attitudes* (Liverpool: Liverpool University Press), pp. 78–93.

Key, V.O. (1966) *The Responsible Electorate* (New York: Vintage).

Komito, L. & Gallagher, M. (2010) The constituency role of Dáil deputies, in: J. Coakley & M. Gallagher (eds) *Politics in the Republic of Ireland* (New York: Routledge), pp. 230–262.

LeDuc, L. and J. Pammett. "The Fate of Governing Parties in Times of Economic Crisis." *Electoral Studies*, 32(3), September 2013, pp. 494–499.

Lowe, Will, Benoit, Kenneth, Mikhaylov, Slava & Laver, Michael (2011) Scaling policy preferences from coded political texts. *Legislative Studies Quarterly*, 36(1), pp. 123–155.

Mair, Peter (1992) Explaining the absence of class politics in Ireland, in: J.H. Goldthorpe & C.T. Whelan (eds) The Development Of Industrial Society In Ireland: The Third Joint Meeting Of The Royal Irish Academy And The British Academy, Oxford: Oxford University Press/British Academy, pp. 383–410.

Mair, Peter (2011) The election in context, in: Michael Gallagher and Michael Marsh (eds) *How Ireland Voted 2011: The Full Story of Ireland's Earthquake Election* (Basingstoke: Palgrave), pp. 283–297.

Marsh, Michael (2007) Candidates or parties? Objects of electoral choice in Ireland. *Party Politics*, 13(4), pp. 500–527.

Marsh, Michael & Cunningham, Kevin (2011) A positive choice, or anyone but Fianna Fáil? in: Michael Gallagher & Michael Marsh (eds) *How Ireland Voted 2011: The Full Story of Ireland's Earthquake Election* (Basingstoke: Palgrave), pp. 172–202.

Marsh, Michael & Mikhaylov, Slava (2012) Economic voting in a crisis: the Irish election of 2011. *Electoral Studies*, 31(3), pp. 478–484.

Marsh, Michael & Tilley, James (2010) The attribution of credit and blame to governments and its impact on vote choice. *British Journal of Political Science*, 40(1), pp. 115–134.

Marsh, Michael, Sinnott, Richard, Garry, John & Kennedy, Fiachra (2008) *The Irish Voter: The Nature of Electoral Competition in the Republic of Ireland* (Manchester: Manchester University Press).

Miller, W. & Shanks, M. (1996) *The New American Voter* (Cambridge, MA: Harvard University Press).

Powell, G. Bingham & Whitten, Guy D. (1993) A cross-national analysis of economic voting: taking account of the political context. *American Journal of Political Science*, 37, pp. 391–414.

Sacks, Paul (1976) *The Donegal Mafia: An Irish Political Machine* (New Haven and London: Yale University Press).

Sinnott, Richard (1995) *Irish Voters Decide: Voting Behaviour in Elections and Referendums since 1918* (Manchester: Manchester University Press).

Stokes, D.E. (1963) Spatial models of party competition. *American Journal of Political Science*, 57(2), pp. 368–377.

Suiter, Jane & Farrell, David (2011) The parties' manifestos, in: Michael Gallagher & Michael Marsh (eds) *How Ireland Voted 2011: The Full Story of Ireland's Earthquake Election* (Basingstoke: Palgrave), pp. 29–46.

The Elections of the Great Recession in Portugal: Performance Voting under a Blurred Responsibility for the Economy

PEDRO C. MAGALHÃES
University of Lisbon, Portugal

ABSTRACT *This article discusses the basic patterns of voting behaviour in the most recent elections in Portugal. These elections were fought under one of the most profound economic crises in the country's four decades of democracy, after a bailout agreement with the EU and the IMF, and under an unusually high level of campaign polarization around the issues of economic austerity and liberalization. First, the article examines whether this context ended up being favourable to "performance" voting or, instead, to an enhanced importance of position issues, particularly those related to the role of the state in the economy and welfare provision. Second, it examines how the context of the Great Recession and the European sovereign debt crisis created opportunities for incumbents to use blame-shifting and blame-sharing strategies, and the extent to which voters' ambivalence about who to hold responsible for the sorry state of the economy was consequential for vote choices, either by directly affecting them or by moderating the relationship between economic perceptions and the vote.*

Introduction

The 2011 legislative elections in Portugal took place under one of the most acute economic crises ever faced by the country in four decades of democracy. To be sure, all general elections in Portugal since at least 1999 have taken place under some sort of economic distress, often compounded by (and manifesting itself in) acute political crises. However, the sheer magnitude of the economic problems faced this time was rather different from those that characterized the preceding elections. Unlike what was occurring in 2011 with many European economies, which were by then slowly recovering from the worst moments of the Great Recession, the Portuguese economy had become a disaster zone. GDP was still contracting, the unemployment rate was already above 12% – the highest since reliable statistics have been collected – and consumer confidence had reached the lowest level ever recorded. By the end of 2010, central government debt represented 93% of GDP, and the budget deficit reached almost 10% of GDP, the largest in more than a century. To top it all, in April 2011, the Socialist (minority) government was forced to admit that the country had become unable to meet debt obligations, requesting financial rescue from the EU and the IMF. The memorandum of agreement signed between the Portuguese government and the so-called "troika" (the European Commission, the European Central Bank, and the International Monetary Fund) on 3 May 2011, which allowed Portugal access to a €78 billion bailout, contained a long and detailed list of measures aiming at deficit reduction that any future government would have to implement. This agreement, which involved not only the government's Socialist Party (PS) but also two other opposition parties, the Social-Democratic Party (PSD, centre-right) and the Social and Democratic Centre-Popular Party (CDS-PP, right), included cuts in public sector wages and jobs, reductions in the costs of health, education, and state-owned enterprises, cuts in pensions and unemployment benefits, tax increases, and a large privatization programme. The next elections were just around the corner, to be held on 5 June.

What to expect from elections held in such a context? The simplest expectation would be that, in a context of such profound economic crisis and the failure of government to prevent a financial bailout, voters would punish the Socialist incumbents quite severely. After all, just a few months earlier, in what seemed like a very similar context – economic crisis, impending default, and an EU/IMF rescue – the February 2011 elections in Ireland had caused Fianna Fáil to lose no less than 24 percentage points of the vote and more than two-thirds of the seats it previously held in parliament. It has been argued, more generally, that the disastrous fate of many incumbents in the elections of the Great Recession is explained by these sorts of performance considerations: "in periods of economic crisis, as in more normal times, voters have a strong tendency to support any policies that seem to work, and to punish leaders regardless of their ideology when economic growth is slow" (Bartels, 2012: 50).

However, other aspects of the electoral context generated complementary and, in some cases, competing expectations. First, the austerity measures to which Portugal had committed in the bailout agreement and other not so inevitable ones proposed during the campaign turned out to be a very salient element of the election. The PSD, the main centre-right opposition party, had made since 2010, under the new leadership of Pedro Passos Coelho, a rather decisive turn vis-à-vis openly liberal and "market-friendly" economic policies, and promised during the campaign that the PSD's government platform would go "beyond the troika" in "reforming education, justice, health, and social security" and ensuring a "transformation of the country."[1] Conversely, the Socialists advanced growth-promoting public investment and spending as a way out of the crisis, and denounced PSD's proposals as representing nothing less than the destruction of the Portuguese welfare state. This surprising – for Portuguese standards – level of ideological polarization of the campaign around economic and social welfare policy themes seemed to create a context in which position issues, particularly around privatization, welfare provision, and the overall role of the state in economy and society, could have played an important role in the election, beyond considerations about sanctioning or rewarding economic and governmental performance.

Second, although Portugal's economic crisis was certainly one of the most acute in Europe, the country was not alone in this regard. Greece and Ireland were already either under bailout agreements and Italy and Spain's public accounts were already and increasingly under scrutiny. More generally, the European crisis initiated in 2007/2008 has highlighted the current deep integration of the international economy and the numerous agents and forces potentially responsible for outcomes, including international and supranational institutions, rating agencies, foreign governments, and banks. In the case of Portugal in 2011, the potential blurring of responsibility this already entailed was compounded by the particular sequence of events that led to the bailout just before the election, and by the way those events created further opportunities for domestic political actors to shift or share blame for what was almost unanimously seen as a disastrous economic situation. The literature has pointed out several potential consequences of these kinds of processes. First, independently of how negative the perceptions of the economic and political situations may be among the public, voters may make rather different judgments about who is responsible for them, and such judgments may have themselves direct consequences on vote choices (Hellwig & Coffey, 2011). Second, if perceptions of political control of the economy become more diffuse, the relationship between domestic performance and vote choices may become weaker (Fernández-Albertos, 2006; Hellwig & Samuels, 2007). For example, voters who tend to blame the European Union for the economic situation of the country may be less likely to punish domestic incumbents for negative outcomes (Lobo & Lewis-Beck, 2012). Finally, it has even been argued that, in such contexts, voters may be led to "compensate for the loss of political control in certain areas by reemphasizing other policy areas (noneconomic issues)" (Hellwig, 2008: 1139). Do the Portuguese 2011 elections provide evidence supporting any of these hypotheses?

This article is divided in three sections. The next section discusses the economic and political context of the 2011 election in Portugal, comparing it to that of the previous elections. Then, I look at the determinants of voting choices for the four major parties in Portugal. Broadly speaking, models of vote choice tend to focus on three major factors (Hellwig, 2008: 1128): performance evaluations, policy positions, and nonpolicy factors (such as partisan attachments, for example). Here, I look particularly at how performance considerations – linked to evaluations of the economy and to evaluations of the performance of the incumbent in various domains – compare with policy positions in terms of the role in vote choices, also comparing the 2011 elections with previous ones. Finally, I address the themes of perceived responsibility for economic outcomes and EU issue voting. Was the predictable punishment that the incumbent was likely to suffer somehow mitigated by the complex assignment of political responsibility for outcomes on the part of voters? And in what way(s)?

The Context of the 2011 Elections

The Economy and Government Performance

The description of the basic aspects of the economic and political performance at the time of the 2011 elections, both objectively and as subjectively perceived by voters, reads as a litany of disasters for the incumbent party in Portugal. To be sure, this is not entirely new in recent Portuguese history. However, as Table 1 shows, it was always possible to find, here and there, some sort of mitigating circumstance in previous elections. In 2002, for example, the economy was still growing above the European average and unemployment remained remarkably low. In 2005, the economy was still growing (although now at a slower pace than in the rest of the EU) and unemployment remained below the EU average. In 2009, the economy's violent contraction was, after all, not as dramatic as in most European countries, while economic sentiment also remained less pessimistic than in the rest of the continent. By 2011, however, no redeeming circumstances were available: real GDP growth in Portugal remained negative while many European countries were already recovering; unemployment reached record levels; the budget deficit was now close to 10% of GDP; and economic sentiments had failed to improve since 2009, in contrast with what had occurred in the rest of Europe.

Accordingly, public evaluations of the economy also had also reached a low point around the time of the 2011 elections. In the 2011 post-election survey, 57% of respondents believed that their personal economic situation had become "Worse" or "Much worse" in the last year, while no less than 94% responded in the same way when asked about the situation of the national economy.[2] Although retrospective evaluations of voters' personal economic situation were not much worse in 2011 than around the previous three elections, retrospective sociotropic perceptions – typically

Table 1. The economic context of elections in Portugal since 2002

Elections	March 2002	February 2005	September 2009	June 2011
Real GDP growth in previous four quarters	1.7%	1.1%	−3.6%	−0.6%
EU 27 average	1.5%	2.0%	−5.3%	2.3%
Unemployment rate in month before election	4.8%	8.1%	11.1%	12.7%
EU 27 average	8.8%	9.2%	9.3%	9.5%
Budget deficit (% of GDP) in year before election	−4.3%	−3.4%	−3.6%	−9.8%
EU 27 average	−1.9%	−2.9%	−2.1%	−6.2%
Economic sentiment indicator in month before election	100.4	96.3	87.0	87.2
EU 27 average	96.3	103.6	84.3	104.9

Source: Eurostat.

the most consequential in terms of voting choices (Lewis-Beck & Stegmaier, 2000) – had deteriorated quite dramatically in comparison with previous election surveys.[3] Evaluations of government performance were also at a particularly low point for the Socialist incumbents by 2011. A full 80% of the respondents in the Portuguese Election Study thought the government had done, in terms of overall performance, "Badly" or "Very badly" during its tenure, clearly worse than in 2009. Looking at specific areas – education, health, welfare, justice – no redeeming points could be identified, and evaluations of economic management were particularly negative.

This combination of factors seemed to spell doom for the Socialist incumbent, especially considering what the existing research on electoral behaviour tends to emphasize about Portuguese voters. First, Portuguese parties, particularly the centre-left PS and the centre-right PSD, are "among the most weakly anchored in Europe in terms of class and religious determinants of the vote", giving them, as incumbent parties, a low level of cushioning against economic crises, and making levels of electoral volatility in Portugal among the highest in the advanced democracies (Gunther, 2005: 272). Second, such low social anchoring of the vote seems not to be compensated by high and stable levels of partisanship. Instead, less than half of Portuguese voters report being close to any party (Huber et al., 2005). Finally, performance judgments and sanctioning mechanisms seem, historically, to play a particularly strong role in determining voting choices. Whether evaluations of government performance or retrospective evaluations of the economy should be seen as taking primacy as the most potent predictors of vote choices seems to depend largely, in the extant literature, on options concerning model specification and other methodological choices (Freire, 2004; Freire & Lobo, 2005; Magalhães, 2007). However, from any of these perspectives – perceptions of economic or government performance – the prospects for the Socialists in 2011 seemed equally grim.

Position Issues and Party Discourse

The expectations about the extent to which voting choices in 2011 were also likely to be affected by position issues, on either economic or non-economic policy, were less clear. Traditionally, both the Socialists and the centre-right PSD (confusingly but tellingly called "Social Democratic Party") could be reliably counted among the most moderate, respectively, centre-left and centre-right forces among European party systems. Analysts have traditionally noted the lack of ideological differentiation between the main alternatives in Portugal's party system ("the Central Bloc"), their nature as "catch-all" or even "cartel" parties, and their pragmatic appeals to a centrist "marais" electorate (Biezen, 2003; Jalali, 2007).

However, an observer of the 2011 election campaign and its antecedents would have difficulty in recognizing Portugal in these descriptions. Already in April 2010, Pedro Passos Coelho, fresh from his victory in the PSD primaries, announced that the party would propose several constitutional amendments aimed at "reducing the role of the state in society" and "increasing people's ability to make choices in health and education".[4] Those included eliminating the expression "tend to be free of charge" in reference to the National Health Service and public education and changing the "fair cause" limitation in what concerned the ability to dismiss workers, just to mention some of the most contentious issues. For the 2011 election, the PSD's electoral platform proposed a "change of the current statist paradigm", criticizing the PS government for having adopted a "wrong model of development ... based on the continuous increase of the weight and size of the State".[5]

This dislocation to the right of the PSD (in which it was also followed by the CDS) is clearly visible when we look at party manifesto data. To construct Figure 1, I resorted to the Manifesto Project database (Volkens et al., 2012) and computed, for each of the four major parties in all elections since 2005, a variation of the measure proposed by Kim and Fording (1998), as applied to the original categories of manifesto statements used by Laver and Budge (1992) to measure the left–right positions of parties, restricting myself, in this case, to economic policy categories.[6] That measure, PEP (Party economic position) ranges from -1 to 1, with -1 as the leftmost position and 1 as the rightmost position, and is computed as:

$$PEP = \frac{\sum \%Pro - Right\ statements - \sum \%Pro - Left\ statements}{\sum \%Pro - Right\ statements + \sum \%Pro - Left\ statements}$$

Figure 1 shows a clear increase in the ideological polarization of party discourse in the Portuguese party system in 2011, driven both by a shift of the Communist Party to the left and an even more decisive shift of both the PSD and the CDS to the right. Although the analysis of the Socialists' manifesto also denounces a smaller shift to the economic right, messages supporting welfare expansion and market regulation were still dominant in the PS's discourse. Throughout the campaign, the Socialists

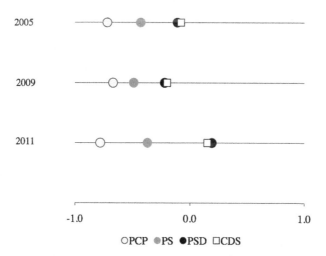

Figure 1. Party positions on economic policies on the basis of manifesto data.

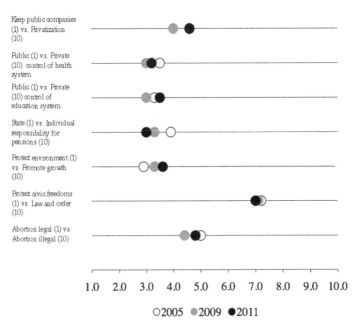

Figure 2. Sample means of ten-point issue scales. Portuguese Election Study 2005–2011.

kept denouncing the PSD as a party composed by "conservatives" and "neo-liberals" set on dismantling the Portuguese welfare state,[7] accusing the PSD of "ideological radicalism" and of intending to destroy the National Health Service and the public education system.[8]

The rightward shift of the PSD and the CDS in this election was particularly striking, as it represented a shift away from the central tendencies of the Portuguese electorate in terms of economic policy positions. Figure 2 shows the sample mean positions of the respondents in the 2005, 2009 and 2011 post-election surveys on seven ten-point issue scales, where the extremes were labelled with contrasting positions.[9] The first four issue scales are related to the role of the state in the economy (public ownership of companies vs. privatization) or in the provision of welfare (health, education, pensions). The remaining issue scales are related to "protection of the environment" vs. "promote growth by lifting environmental restrictions", "maintain law and order" vs. "protect civic freedoms" and "keep abortion legal" vs. "making abortion always illegal". In the "law and order" issue, Portuguese voters do tend to espouse right-of-centre views. However, on economic policy issues, those positions have remained mostly unchanged in last years, and are mostly to the left. Although mean positions on privatization tend approach the centre of the scale, they are still left-of-centre, and more than 50% of respondents could be found in the first four points of the scale in the 2011 survey. In the other issues related to the state's role in the economy and on welfare provision, the mean positions of the Portuguese electorate are even more decidedly leftist.

The question, therefore, was whether this would make any difference for voting choices. Previous studies had shown that, in spite of the pre-eminence of performance voting in Portugal, the choice between leftist and rightist parties, at least in 2005, was also linked to voters' views about welfare policies and the role of the state in the economy (Freire, 2009: 215). The 2011 elections, fought under the shadow of a troika memorandum that included harsh austerity measures and of an increased polarization of party discourse around economic policies, seemed to provide an even better opportunity for position issues to leave their mark in voting choices. Was this really the case?

Position Issues and Performance Evaluations in the 2011 Election

The 2011 election did bring an important punishment for the incumbent party. The Socialists in power lost more than eight points vis-à-vis the 2009 election, ending up with 29.3% of the vote, their worst score in more than two decades. Their main centre-right opponents, the PSD, obtained 40.3% of the valid vote, 11 points ahead of the Socialists. The CDS-PP obtained its best score since 1983–12.2% of the valid vote. The Communists basically kept their previous electoral support and, among the smaller parties represented in parliament, only the left-libertarian Leftist Bloc (BE) experienced major losses, from 10% to 5% (see Magalhães, 2012, for a more detailed account).

These aggregate results, however, are not enough to tell us how and why voters behaved the way they did, particularly in what concerns the importance of performance voting vs. position issues, and in comparison with previous elections. To elucidate this, using the 2005, 2009 and 2011 post-election surveys, I estimated multinomial logit models where the dependent variable was coded 1 if the respondent voted for the main incumbent party (PSD in 2005 and PS in 2009 and 2011), 2 for the main challenger (PS in 2005 and PSD in 2009 and 2011), 3 for the CDS-PP (the party furthest to the right in parliament) and 4 for the CDU (the pre-electoral coalition led by the PCP, the Portuguese Communist Party).

The position issues presented in Figure 2 were included in the models as independent variables, in a simplified manner: I created an average index on "Privatization" averaging positions on the role of the private sector on the economy, health and education, ranging from 1 to 10, with higher values meaning greater support for a smaller role of the state in the economy and welfare provision. The remaining four issue items are separate independent variables, also all ranging from 1 to 10.[10] Then, to capture evaluations of government performance, I created another index averaging evaluations on the different areas of government as well as the overall evaluation of government performance, ranging from 1 to 4.[11] Finally, I include two variables capturing, with five-point scales, retrospective egocentric and sociotropic views about the economy in the last year, i.e, about the recent evolution of the personal and national economy. As control variables, I include age (in number of years), a dummy variable for gender (female), education (in a seven-point scale, from no formal education to college degree or more), religiosity (in a four-point scale, from "not at all religious" to "very religious"), a dummy variable for union membership (for the respondent or anyone else in the household), a four-point scale for "type of neighbourhood" (from "poor" to "rich/upper middle class") as coded by the interviewer,[12] and partisanship, measured as self-reported proximity to the incumbent party, in a three-point scale (from 0, "not close" to 2, "very" or "somewhat close"). Table 2 summarizes the variables employed.

Table 2. Main variables employed in multinomial logit models for the 2005, 2009, and 2011 elections

Dependent variable	Vote: 1, PS; 2, PSD; 3, CDS-PP; 4, CDU
Independent variables	
Socio-demographic	Age; Female; Education (seven-point scale); Religiosity (four-point); Union membership (self or household); Type of neighbourhood (four-point)
Issue position 1: Privatization	Index averaging 1–10 point responses on:
	• "Keep companies public" vs. "Privatize public companies"
	• "State control of health system" vs. "Private control of health system"
	• "State control of education system" vs. "Private control of education system"
Issue position 2: Pensions individual responsibility	1–10 point scale on "State responsibility for pensions" vs. "Individual responsibility for pensions"
Issue position 3: Growth (vs. environment)	1–10 point scale on "Protect the environment" vs. "Promote economic growth"
Issue position 4: Law and order (vs. civic freedoms)	1–10 point scale on "Protect civic freedoms" vs. "Protect law and order"
Issue position 5: Illegal abortion (vs. legal)	1–10 point scale on "Keep abortion legal" vs. "Make abortion illegal"
Partisanship	Three-point scale of proximity to incumbent party
National economy	Five-point scale of evolution of national economy in the last year
Personal economy	Five-point scale of evolution of personal finances in the last year
Government performance	Index averaging four-point scale evaluations of government performance on: • Social policy • Economy • Education • Justice and public safety • Health • Overall

Tables A1 to A3 in the appendix show the estimates of a model where all variables in Table 2 (plus socio-demographic controls) were included simultaneously for each election, 2005, 2009 and 2011. Figures 3 to 6 show the effects of changes in the values of several independent variables in the probability of voting for each of the four major parties. Instead of presenting regression coefficients, the figures show how an increase of one standard deviation in each independent variable, on the basis of the model estimates and when all remaining variables are kept constant at their mean values (mode for Gender – "Female" – and Union membership – "Non member"), is predicted to affect the probability of voting for each party. Since parties have very different baseline levels of support (including two comparative small parties, the CDS-PP and the CDU), I focus on *proportional change*, i.e. the extent to which an increase of one standard deviation in the value of each independent variable is predicted to increase or decrease vote for each party *in relation to the marginal distribution of the vote in the sample*. So, for example, if party A's baseline level of support is 40% and an increase of one standard deviation in the value of variable X_1 is predicted to increase the probability of voting for that party by 10 percentage points, the effect of variable X_1 (proportional change) is represented here by 10/40, i.e. +0.25. In other words, this is an effect as large as would be an increase of 2.5 percentage points for a party (B) that had received 10% of the vote (2.5/10=0.25). Similarly, if an increase of one standard deviation in the value of X_2 is predicted to decrease the probability of voting for party A by 10 percentage points and the probability of voting for party B by 2.5 percentage points, the predicted proportional change for both parties is -0.25 (-10/40 and -2.5/10). In other words, our measure of effects normalizes the predicted effect of the independent variables by the baseline of the marginal distribution of the vote for each party, thus rendering effects comparable across parties (regardless of their size) and across variables regardless of how they are scaled (since we focus on a one standard deviation increase; for a similar approach, see Carrubba & Timpone, 2005).

Figures 3 and 4 look at the effects of voters' issue positions – on "privatization", pensions, law and order, growth vs. environment, and abortion – on the vote for the four major parties (PS, PSD, CDS-PP and CDU) in the 2005, 2009 and 2011 elections.

The results show, first, that voters' issue positions seem, in general, to have greater effects on the probability of voting for the smaller parties – CDS-PP and CDU – than for the larger incumbent and main challenger parties in each election, the PS and the PSD. This is not surprising: voting for centrist "government" parties – incumbents or those that constitute their main challenger (and who were the main incumbent parties in the recent past) – is less likely to be determined by spatial or "ideological" considerations than by "valence" ones (Clarke et al., 2009: 51–52).

Second, issues about the proper role of the state and the private sector in the economy and in welfare provision seem, in most cases, to have become *less* important as explanations of the vote in 2011 than in previous elections. In fact, in 2011, the actual signs of the coefficients are the opposite of what one would expect, although the effect size is small and not statistically significant. This is rather striking,

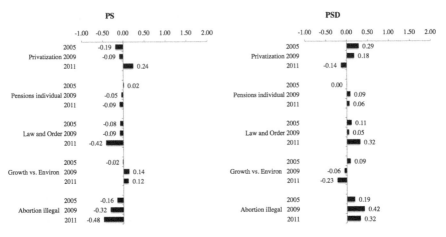

Figure 3. Proportional change in the probability of voting for the PS and the PSD resulting from an increase of one standard deviation in each issue position independent variable while others are kept constant at their mean values (mode for Female and Union membership).

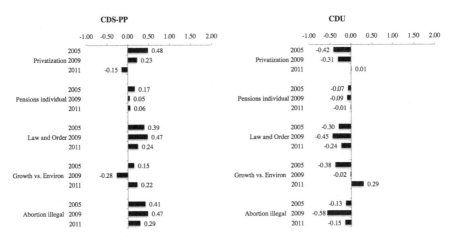

Figure 4. Proportional change in the probability of voting for the CDS-PP and the CDU resulting from an increase of one standard deviation in each issue position independent variable while others are kept constant at their mean values (mode for Female and Union membership).

considering that the general tenor of the election campaign was, as we have seen, one of increasing polarization between parties of the left and of the right around economic and welfare policy issues.

Third, issues related to traditional/conservative views about society (such as an emphasis in law and order vs. civil freedoms or a preference for making abortion illegal) seem to have become *more* important in what concerns the choice for the

PS (in the case of abortion and law and order) and the PSD (law and order). In a related development, our analysis in the appendix also shows that religiosity has become more important in 2011 that in past elections. In 2005, there was simply no relationship between religiosity and vote for the PSD or the PS. By 2011, a one standard deviation increase in the religiosity scale would have decreased the vote for the PS by half, while having the opposite effect in the probability of voting for the PSD. In contrast, as we have seen, the polarization of campaign discourse around the role of the state in the economy and social policies was not reflected on the way voters decided on which party to vote.

Figures 5 and 6 show the results of the components of the model capturing voters' sanctioning mechanisms, namely on the basis of perceptions of government performance and the perceived state of the economy. The results of the economic variables are not very encouraging. Individual perceptions about the evolution of personal finances have been mostly irrelevant for vote choices, with the exception of the decision to vote for the Communist Party: consistently, in the three elections, worse perceptions in that regard increased the probability of voting CDU. The relationships between perceptions of *national* economy and voting are seemingly higher but still of little relevance, and even display the "wrong" sign in the case of the CDU in 2005 and the PSD in 2011 (with a "better" economy favouring opposition parties).

These results should not necessarily lead us to conclude that the state of the economy or the way voters perceived has been irrelevant for vote choices in Portugal. On the one hand, we also recall that, in all three elections, the "national economy" variable exhibited little individual level variance. This is taken to an extreme point in 2011, with only 0.5% of respondents saying the economy had improved in the

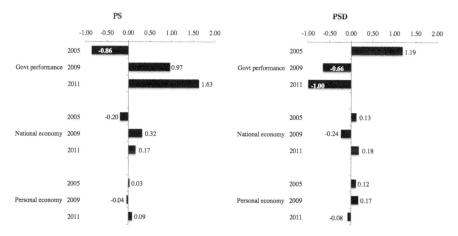

Figure 5. Proportional change in the probability of voting for the PS and the PSD resulting from an increase of one standard deviation in each performance judgment independent variable while others are kept constant at their mean values (mode for Female and Union membership).

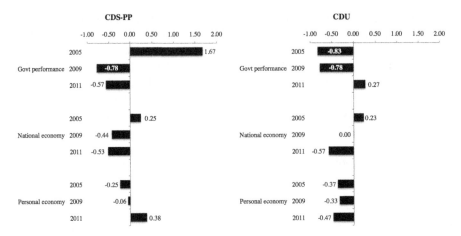

Figure 6. Proportional change in the probability of voting for the CDS-PP and the CDU resulting from an increase of one standard deviation in each performance judgment independent variable while others are kept constant at their mean values (mode for Female and Union membership).

previous year. Thus, if perceived economic performance was to matter at all, it was never so much in terms of how badly things have turned out to be (a highly consensual matter) but rather in terms of who should be held responsible for outcomes (we return to this issue in the next section). Second, there is a considerable amount of work suggesting that the endogeneity of economic perceptions, being themselves explained by partisanship and other measures of support (including, most damagingly, by the vote itself – Evans & Anderson, 2006; Evans & Pickup, 2010), has led, if not taken into account, to overblown estimations of "economic voting". As our model controls for partisanship, and party proximity to the incumbent party is always strongly correlated with retrospective evaluations of the economy in our samples, it is not surprising that the latter end up with little relevance once partisanship is taken into account.[13]

However, as Figures 5 and 6 show, even when controlling for partisanship, the impact of evaluations of government performance are much stronger, showing them as very powerful correlates of voter choices. In 2005, an increase of one standard deviation in the evaluation of government's performance was predicted to more than double the vote for the incumbent parties (at the time, the PSD and the CDS-PP). Very large effects are also present in the 2009 and 2011 elections for the incumbent party, the PS. But even the vote for opposition parties in those two elections, the CDS-PP, the CDU and the PSD (especially in 2011), was strongly linked to performance judgments, and always in the predictable direction (the single exception is the vote for CDU, although the effect is small and not significant). Such effects are invariably larger than those we found for any issue positions in Figures 3 and 4. And the particularly relevant aspect about 2011 is that, although the effects were smaller for the smaller parties, performance evaluations had a much stronger relationship with vote choice for the main incumbent party (the PS, in this case) than in the two previous elections under consideration.

In sum, in spite of the heightened confrontation between the PS and the PSD on the issue of the state's role in the economy and in the provision of welfare and of the PSD's new economically liberal stance on these issues, it does not seem that the 2011 elections were really about that, at least from the voters' point of view. They were mostly about performance and how to sanction or reward the incumbent for it. Unsurprisingly, such effect is particularly visible in the decision to vote for the incumbent Socialists and the main challengers, the PSD. In fact, if the Socialists managed at all to drive a wedge between voters on position issues, such issues were related to traditional/conservative vs. progressive/liberal views of social order, manifested here in the "law and order" and "abortion" issues, which ended up being more consequential than in earlier elections. However, even positions on those issues had a much weaker relationship with the vote than performance evaluations. On the other hand, this also means that the victory of the Social Democrats cannot be interpreted as a electoral mandate to liberalize the Portuguese economy: voters' positions on that issue, as we saw in Figure 2, remained mostly unchanged from 2005 to 2011, and had no impact on voting decisions in the 2011 election.

Why were positions on economic and welfare policy issues of so little relevance, in spite of the increased polarization in party messages in this regard? Tentatively, I suggest that two main factors conspired to produce this outcome. First, besides the fact that the economic crisis was deeper, more evident, and more profound than before, it is after all hard to imagine a clearer certificate of governmental incompetence for the Socialist incumbents than being perceived as having led the country all the way to impending bankruptcy. Thus, performance considerations were always likely to be very available and salient in voters' minds. Second, the credibility of the Socialists as holders of the "welfare protection" or even "welfare expansion" positions was probably quite limited in the eyes of voters. Since 2005, the PS government had adopted a series of policies aimed at reducing the budget deficit inherited from the previous centre-right coalition government, including rationalizing social benefits, delaying the retirement age, and reforming the educational system. These and other measures put the Socialists on a collision course with organized labour, particularly civil servants' and teachers' unions, and ultimately led to a changed perception of where the PS stood ideologically: by 2009, the PS was seen by voters as a fundamentally centrist, rather than leftist, party (Freire, 2010: 595–598). Besides, the 2011 elections took place after the bailout agreement between the Socialist government, the EU and the IMF, which has also been subscribed by the PSD and the CDS-PP. Many of the measures contained in the very detailed memorandum of agreement pointed to a rolling-back of state functions and spending and to a generically market-oriented liberalization. In other words, the basic tenets of the policy endorsed by the PSD, which the Socialists harshly criticized during the campaign were, after all, the same that all major parties, including the PS itself, had committed to implement with the EU and the IMF after the election took place.

Therefore, in this particularly acute context of (imposed) policy convergence, it is understandable that most voters felt that the election was not really about future economic and welfare policies, regardless of what the parties had to say about it during the campaign. Although self-reports of voters' motivations should be taken with more than a grain of salt, it is interesting to look at how respondents answered, in the 2011 survey, to a question on what they thought the election was "really about": 44% responded "the financial crisis", 15% "the lack of economic growth" and 16% about "the right person to lead the country". Although the PS ultimately wished that voters thought the election was about "the survival of the social welfare state", only 6% of respondents agreed.

Who is to Blame, and Does it Matter?

Although voters seem to have paid little heed to differences in parties' discourses on the role of the state in the economy and welfare provision when deciding how to vote, it may be the case that the Socialist government still managed to obtain some respite from the consequences of the crisis in a different fashion: by framing responsibility for the economy as being diffuse and shared by many agents and forces. Since the beginning of the Great Recession, and like many government parties before and since, the PS tried to deflect responsibility for the domestic consequences of the crisis. Throughout this entire period, the government used a variety of arguments to account for negative outcomes. The 2009 budget deficit (-9.3%) and the lack of decisive efforts to diminish it substantially in 2010 were explained by the need to "maintain the stimulus measures necessary for a healthy economic recovery" in the context of a global economic crisis.[14] When downgrades in debt ratings occurred, they were depicted as "unfair" decisions on the part of rating agencies[15] and, later on, as part of a concerted attack by financial markets.[16] Further rises in government bond spreads were assigned to "contagion" from the Greek and Irish bailouts.[17] And so on.

After the 2009 elections, now ruling with a minority government, the PS gained an additional opportunity for blame-sharing, by seeking and obtaining the support of the PSD for two austerity packages during 2010. Besides, the PSD ultimately ended up rejecting a new package in 2011, leading to the resignation of Prime Minister Sócrates, the calling of elections for June, and, ultimately, the "troika" bailout. Given this particular sequence of events, the PS was now able to blame the PSD and Passos Coelho's for their change in position, accusing the party of causing elections for mere political gains and of "throwing the country into the hands of the IMF", thus forcing the country to negotiate a bailout.[18]

Is there any evidence that these efforts registered at all with voters? Did they matter for voting choices, or for the extent to which evaluations of the economy affected those choices? It has been suggested that deeper economic integration and greater economic openness among industrialized economies have affected both the reality and the perception about the influence governments and elections indeed have over economic outcomes and policies, thus creating opportunities for incumbents to exonerate themselves from bad results, weakening the relationship between economic performance and the vote (Fernández-Albertos, 2006; Hellwig, 2001; Hellwig & Samuels, 2007) and raising the impact of non-economic position issues (Hellwig, 2008).[19] Two recent studies illustrate different ways in which assignments of responsibility by voters during the Great Recession may have affected electoral choices. Hellwig and Coffey (2011) show that, independently of evaluations of the state of the economy, perceptions about the responsibility of the British government for the crisis had a direct effect on voting intentions for the 2010 election, with respondents who assigned blame to the Labour government giving a significantly larger edge in terms of voting intentions for the Conservatives, in comparison with those respondents who exonerated the government. Lobo and Lewis-Beck (2012), in turn, discuss an alternative way in which responsibility assignments may affect the vote, by looking at voting intentions in the Southern European countries. They show that, among those respondents who believed the European Union was responsible for economic conditions (or at least among those who believe the EU to be *more* responsible than the national governments), the relationship between perceptions of the economy and voting intentions was weaker.

The results of the 2011 survey allow us to confront these two ideas with the Portuguese evidence. The survey asked a battery of questions about the extent (from 1, "Not at all" to 5, "Extremely responsible") to which the Portuguese government, the European Union, the Euro, the banks, the Bank of Portugal, the international economic situation, the opposition parties and the rating agencies should be seen as "responsible" for the current situation of the economy. The descriptive results start by showing that the electorate was far from unanimous in assigning sole responsibility for the economic situation of the country to the PS government. Overall, although 69% of respondents held the government "very" or "extremely" responsible for the economic situation, nearly half of respondents held similar views about, for example, "the international economic situation", "banks", "rating agencies" or even (for 47% of respondents) the European Union.

The next question is whether this mattered for the vote. I first created an index averaging the values of the "responsibility for the economy" variables for all actors and forces with the exception of the government. Then, I computed a new variable, by subtracting the values of the above-mentioned index to the variable measuring perceptions of government responsibility for the economy. Since the original variables are coded in five-point scales, this new variable (*Government's exclusive responsibility*) ranges from -4 (a respondent who finds all other actors "extremely responsible" and the government "not at all responsible") to 4 (a respondent who finds the government "extremely responsible" and all other actors "not at all responsible"), with the value 0 meaning that respondents found the government and non-government actors equally responsible (or equally not responsible). The mean value for this variable is 0.42, suggesting that, on average, voters tended to assign greater responsibility to the government, but also that such assignment was not exclusive for most voters. I included this variable in the expanded multinomial logit model showed in Table A4 in the appendix. Furthermore, that model also includes a variable measuring perceived responsibility of the EU for the economic crisis, as well as its interaction with

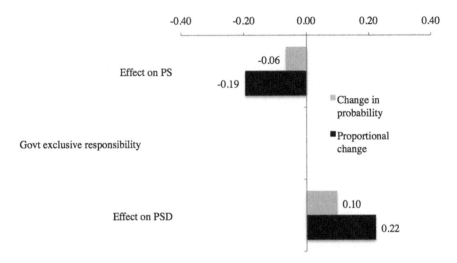

Figure 7. Change in probability and proportional change in probability of voting for the PS and the PSD resulting from an increase of one standard deviation in views about the government's exclusive responsibility for the economy.

retrospective evaluations of the economy, testing the hypothesis that assignments of responsibility to the European Union conditioned the relationship between evaluations of the economy and vote choices.

The results show, first, that the coefficient for the *Government exclusive responsibility* variable is significant for the contrast between the PS and the PSD. Figure 7 shows both the predicted net change and the proportional change in the probability of voting for the PS and the PSD that results from an increase of one standard deviation in the *Government exclusive responsibility* variable.

The extent to which voters attributed exclusive responsibility for the economy to the government indeed made a difference: it increased significantly the probability of voting for the PSD and diminished the probability of voting for the incumbent Socialists. The proportional change is clearly much smaller than that associated with evaluations of government performance, as we could see in Figure 5, but it is nevertheless relevant. The second hypothesis, following Lobo and Lewis-Beck (2012), is that assignments of responsibility to the European Union may have conditioned the relationship between perceptions of the economy and vote choices. It is well known that direct readings of the coefficients for the constitutive elements of interaction terms, which we can see in Table A4, can be very deceptive (Brambor et al., 2006). Therefore, I estimated the effects of the *Retrospective national economy* variable on the probability of voting for the incumbent under different values of the *EU responsibility for the economy* variable. Although the results show that the point estimates of the marginal effect of economic evaluations decrease as the perceived *EU responsibility* increases. However, those marginal effects, even when the EU is seen as blameless, are never statistically significant.

In sum, the evidence falls more in favour of a direct relationship between respon-sibility judgments on the vote than of its moderating role on the relationship between economic perceptions and the vote. To be sure, as it occurred with economic evalu-ations, attributions of responsibility are also potentially endogenous, determined themselves by partisanship and other aspects of political support (Tilley & Hobolt, 2011). Simply including partisanship as a control, as it has been done here, is insuffi-cient to fully address this problem. However, the evidence available does favour the conjecture that the Socialist government has been able to frame, near a relevant number of voters, the responsibility for the economic situation as being shared with other agents and forces, and, by doing so, to succeed in mitigating both its own electoral losses and the as gains for the main opposition party.

Conclusion

Incumbents in the industrialized democracies have endured severe electoral punish-ments since the beginning of the Great Recession. Portugal is certainly no exception to this pattern, as the Socialist incumbents had one of their worse electoral perform-ances ever in the 2011 elections. But how should this severe punishment be read in light of what we could find out in terms of the determinants of voting choices in these elections? As the normal punishment any incumbent would endure under a very severe economic crisis and a very public demonstration of mismanagement, such as the EU/IMF bailout? As a rejection of left-wing expansionist policies or, instead, of austerity policies advocated by the right? Or as a smaller punishment than what might be endured in normal circumstances, given a particular situation where economic interdependence and the "European" or even "global" nature of the crisis was more evident than in other occasions?

The results suggest two complementary readings. First, in 2011, as before, per-formance evaluations and the sanctioning of incumbents on the basis of bad evalu-ations were overwhelmingly more important in driving voter choices than position issues concerning welfare policies and the role of the state in the economy. Further-more, in spite of the higher polarization on party discourse in this respect that seems to have characterized the Portuguese 2011 elections, economic policy position issues seem to have been even less relevant than in past elections on which we have data. We must keep in mind the particular setting of the Portuguese elections. On the one hand, a country brought to the verge of bankruptcy under the stewardship of a single-party government that had been in power since 2005, highlighting competence issues to the extreme. On the other hand, a Socialist party whose credibility to drive a wedge between "left" and "right" in this respect was rather limited, given both its past policies and a bailout agreement that the government itself had signed. It may be the case that these patterns are not replicated in elections in other countries under severe economic crisis. For example, if elections take place after the consequences of harsh austerity policies have already been fully felt or in political contexts where policy divergence between parties has been more credibly politicized, the potential for pos-ition issues to emerge as relevant is higher. Having said that, the results for Portugal do little to disconfirm the notion that the punishments endured by governments during the Great Recession have been less about condoning or rejecting particular economic policies than they were about condoning or rejecting governments mostly on the basis of their immediate successes or failures (Bartels, 2012).

Second, the results also point to the importance of taking into account that such successes and failures may be hard to assign unambiguously in a context of heightened economic interdependence, and particularly so in the context of the recent economic, financial and political crisis in Europe. Although most voters blamed the Socialist government for the economic situation, the context of the Great Recession and of the sovereign debt crisis, as well as the particular sequence of events around the Portuguese bailout, seem to have led a considerable amount of voters to assign responsibility to other agents and forces. Some were identifiable, such as the opposition parties. Others were impersonal or outside the control of domestic actors, such as the pace of the international economy or the role of rating agencies. In any case, such assignments were significantly related with vote choices, and may have served to mitigate the losses the Socialists were likely to experience on performance judgments alone. And as Hellwig (2008) suggests should happen in contexts of lower perceived domestic control of the economy, noneconomic issues made somewhat of a resurgence in the Portuguese elections. All this, together with evidence from other studies in other countries (Hellwig & Coffey, 2011; Lobo & Lewis-Beck, 2012), suggests that the context of the Great Recession may have also provided opportunities for blame-shifting and blame-sharing that contributed to counterbalance, if just partially, the relationship between the performance of incumbents and the extent of their electoral punishment.

Notes

1. "Passos Coelho diz que Governo pode ir além das medidas da troika", *Público*, 6 June 2011, available at <http://economia.publico.pt/Noticia/passos-coelho-diz-que-governo-pode-ir-alem-das-medidas-da-troika_1497781>.

2. The Portuguese 2011 post-election survey was conducted between 8 and 28 July 2011, through a CAPI, in person, face-to-face survey, of a random sample of registered voters in primary sampling points stratified by region and size of locality. 1,000 interviews were completed, with a response rate of 62%.

3. The 2005 post-election survey was conducted between 5 March and 5 May 2005, through a PAPI, in person, face-to-face survey, to a random sample of registered voters in primary sampling points stratified by region and size of locality. 2,801 interviews were completed, with a response rate of 31%. The 2009 post-election survey was conducted between 2 October 2009 and 8 February 2010, through a PAPI, in person, face-to-face survey, to a random sample of registered voters in primary sampling points stratified by region and size of locality. 1,317 interviews were completed, with a response rate of 36%. All results available with the author.

4. Patrícia Pires and Sara Marques, "Vamos rever a Constituição e vamos revê-la depressa", *TVI*, 11 April 2010, available at <http://alturl.com/a2jrd>.

5. "Passos Coelho quer 'mudar actual paradigma estatizante'", *Diário de Notícias*, 29 March 2011, available at <http://alturl.com/ywd3j>.

6. Namely, per401 (Free enterprise), per402 (Incentives), per407 (Negative proteccionism), per414 (Economic orthodoxy), and per505 (Welfare state limitation) as "pro-right" statements, and per403

(Market regulation), per404 (Economic planning), per406 (Protectionism positive), per412 (Controlled economy), per413 (Nationalization), per504 (Welfare state expansion), and per 506 (Education expansion), as "pro-left" statements.

7. Leonete Botelho and Nuno Simas, "Assis abre jornadas do PS com críticas à proposta de revisão constitucional do PSD", *Público*, 5 July 2010, available at <http://alturl.com/ytedk>.

8. See "Sócrates acusa PSD de querer 'destruir o Serviço Nacional de Saúde'". *Jornal de Notícias*, 7 May 2011, available at <http://alturl.com/kghe7>; and Carla Soares, "Sócrates acusa PSD de querer desviar verbas da escola pública para a privada", *Jornal de Notícias*, 8 May 2011, available at <http://alturl.com/drjot>.

9. These were the issues scales that were common to the three surveys, and we dropped the 2002 survey from the analysis due to lack of comparable issue scales. We recoded the data so that presumably "leftist" positions have the lowest scores while "rightist" positions have the highest scores.

10. Factor analysis of the seven issue scales in the three election surveys shows that only positions on privatization of companies and the role of the private sector in health and education consistently emerge as loading strongly in a single factor.

11. Factor analysis of the performance variables shows that, in the three surveys, all of them load strongly in a single factor.

12. The inclusion of the "type of neighborhood" variable attempts to adresses the problem of low item response rates (reaching 50% in one of the surveys) to the household income question. The lowest correlation between the "type of neighborhood" and the household income scales in any of the surveys is 0.42.

13. Having said that, others have argued that efforts to capture the effect of economic perceptions independently of partisanship may be a futile endeavour, as "economic voting is one path by which partisan debates are expressed in the electorate" (Stevenson & Duch, 2013: 319). We take no sides in this controversy here, except to recognize that, from this point of view, our model does tend to "stack the deck" against finding effects of economic perceptions.

14. Sócrates reúne com imprensa estrangeira para defender méritos do novo Orçamento, available at <http://www.jornaldenegocios.pt/home.php?template=SHOWNEWS_V2&id=407027>.

15. Sócrates considera injusta a decisão da S&P de colocar o rating de Portugal sob revisão, available at <http://www.oje.pt/noticias/economia/socrates-considera-injusta-a-decisao-da-sp-de-colocar-o-rating-de-portugal-sob-revisao>.

16. "Portugal causa mercados financeiros de atacarem economia nacional", available at <http://pt.euronews.com/2010/04/28/portugal-acusa-mercados-financeiros-de-atacarem-economia-nacional/>.

17. "Portugal nega que será o próximo a pedir socorro financeiro", available at <http://www.dw.de/dw/article/0,,6258786,00.html>.

18. E. Miranda, "Sócrates acusa PSD de querer FMI e crise política", *Jornal de Negócios*, 15 March 2011, available at <http://alturl.com/sycmj>.

19. But see also Vowles (2008) showing that indices of globalization have little relation with perceptions about whether "who is in power makes a difference".

References

Bartels, L.M. (2012) Elections in hard times. *Juncture*, 19(1), pp. 44–50.

Biezen, I. van (2003) *Political Parties in New Democracies: Party Organization in Southern and East-Central Europe* (Basingstoke and New York: Palgrave Macmillan).

Brambor, T., Clark, W.R. & Golder, M. (2006) Understanding interaction models: improving empirical analyses. *Political Analysis*, 14(1), pp. 63–82.

Carrubba, C. & Timpone, R.J. (2005) Explaining vote switching across first-and second-order elections. *Comparative Political Studies*, 38(3), pp. 260–281.

Clarke, H.D., Sanders, D., Stewart, Marianne C. & Whiteley, Paul F. (2009) *Performance Politics and the British Voter* (Cambridge: Cambridge University Press).

Evans, G. & Anderson, R. (2006) The political conditioning of economic perceptions. *Journal of Politics*, 68(1), pp. 194–207.

Evans, G. & Pickup, M. (2010) Reversing the causal arrow: the political conditioning of economic perceptions in the 2000–2004 U.S. presidential election cycle. *Journal of Politics*, 72(4), pp. 1236–1251.

Fernández-Albertos, J. (2006) Does internationalisation blur responsibility? Economic voting and economic openness in 15 European countries. *West European Politics*, 29(1), pp. 28–46.

Freire, A. (2004) Issue voting in Portugal: the 2002 legislative elections. *West European Politics*, 27(5), pp. 779–800.

Freire, A. (2009) Valores, temas e voto em Portugal, 2005 e 2006: analisando velhas questões com nova evidência, in: M. Costa Lobo & P.C. Magalhães (eds) *As Eleições Legislativas e Presidenciais, 2005–2006* (Lisbon: Imprensa de Ciências Sociais), pp. 183–224.

Freire, A. (2010) A new era in democratic Portugal? The 2009 European, legislative and local elections. *South European Society and Politics*, 15(4), pp. 593–613.

Freire, A. & Lobo, M.C. (2005) Economics, ideology and vote: Southern Europe, 1985–2000. *European Journal of Political Research*, 44(4), pp. 493–518.

Gunther, R. (2005) Parties and electoral behavior in Southern Europe. *Comparative Politics*, 253–275.

Hellwig, T. (2001) Interdependence, government constraints, and economic voting. *Journal of Politics*, 63(4), pp. 1141–1162.

Hellwig, T. (2008) Globalization, policy constraints, and vote choice. *The Journal of Politics*, 70(4), pp. 1128–1141.

Hellwig, T. & Coffey, E. (2011) Public opinion, party messages, and responsibility for the financial crisis in Britain. *Electoral Studies*, 30(3), pp. 417–426.

Hellwig, T. & Samuels, D. (2007) Voting in open economies. *Comparative Political Studies*, 40(3), pp. 283–306.

Huber, J.D., Kernell, G. & Leoni, E.L. (2005) Institutional context, cognitive resources and party attachments across democracies. *Political Analysis*, 13(4), pp. 365–386.

Jalali, C. (2007) The same old cleavages? Old cleavages and new values, in: A. Freire, M.C. Lobo & P.C. Magalhães (eds) *Portugal at the Polls* (Lanham: Lexington Books), pp. 49–70.

Kim, H.M. & Fording, R.C. (1998) Voter ideology in western democracies, 1946–1989. *European Journal of Political Research*, 33, pp. 73–97.

Laver, M. & Budge, I. (eds) (1992) *Party Policy and Coalition Government* (New York: St. Martin's Press).

Lewis-Beck, M.S. & Stegmaier, M. (2000) Economic determinants of election outcomes. *Annual Review of Political Science*, 3, pp. 183–219.

Lobo, M.C. & Lewis-Beck, M.S. (2012) The integration hypothesis: how the European Union shapes economic voting. *Electoral Studies*, 31(3), pp. 522–528.

Magalhães, P.C. (2007) What are (semi) presidential elections about? A case study of the Portuguese 2006 elections. *Journal of Elections, Public Opinion and Parties*, 17(3), pp. 263–291.

Magalhães, P.C. (2012) Portugal: responsibility, policy, and valence in a "post-bailout" election. *South European Society and Politics*, 17(2), pp. 309–327.

Stevenson, R.E. & Duch, R. (2013) The meaning and use of subjective perceptions in studies of economic voting. *Electoral Studies*, 32, pp. 305–320.

Tilley, J. & Hobolt, S.B. (2011) Is the government to blame? An experimental test of how partisanship shapes perceptions of performance and responsibility. *Journal of Politics*, 73(2), pp. 316–330.

Volkens, A., Lehmann, P., Merz, N., Regel, S. & Werner, A. (2012) *The Manifesto Data Collection: Manifesto Project (MRG/CMP/MARPOR)* (Berlin: Wissenschaftszentrum Berlin für Sozialforschung).

Vowles, J. (2008) Does globalization affect public perceptions of "who in power can make a difference"? Evidence from 40 countries, 1996–2006. *Electoral Studies*, 27, pp. 63–76.

Appendix

Table A1. Multinomial logit analysis of the vote in the 2005 elections in Portugal. PSD (main incumbent party) as the reference category

	PS	CDS-PP	CDU
Female	−0.08 (0.23)	−0.19 (0.28)	−0.25 (0.30)
Age	−0.009 (0.007)	0.02 (0.009)	−0.02 (0.01)
Religiosity	−0.27 (0.16)	−0.26 (0.20)	−0.92 (0.21)***
Education	−0.005 (0.08)	0.19 (0.10)	−0.09 (0.12)
Union membership	0.48 (0.27)	−0.32 (0.38)	1.03 (0.34)**
Type of neighbourhood	0.09 (0.16)	0.27 (0.21)	−0.19 (0.21)
Partisanship incumbent	−2.47 (0.24)***	−1.51 (0.22)***	−2.26 (0.51)***
Privatization	−0.13 (0.05)*	0.005 (0.06)	−0.20 (0.08)**
Pensions individual responsibility	0.005 (0.04)	0.05 (0.04)	−0.10 (0.06)
Growth vs. protection of environment	−0.03 (0.05)	0.003 (0.05)	−0.12 (0.07)
Law and order vs. civic freedoms	−0.04 (0.04)	0.03 (0.06)	−0.10 (0.05)
Abortion illegal vs. legal	−0.06 (0.03)	0.01 (0.04)	−0.06 (0.04)
Retrospective personal economy	−0.09 (0.17)	−0.26 (0.21)	−0.41 (0.22)
Retrospective national economy	−0.19 (0.13)	0.06 (0.15)	0.11 (0.17)
Government performance	−1.92 (0.23)***	−0.12 (0.26)	−2.15 (0.29)***
Intercept	8.27 (1.05)***	−0.33 (1.24)	−2.15 (0.29)***
N		1,204	
Pseudo R-squared (McFadden)		0.36	

Notes: *p<0.5; **p<0.01; ***p<0.001. Robust standard errors in parentheses.

Table A2. Multinomial logit analysis of the vote in the 2009 elections in Portugal. PS (main incumbent party) as the reference category

	PSD	CDS-PP	CDU
Female	−0.34 (0.29)	−.038 (0.37)	−0.54 (0.36)
Age	0.02 (0.009)*	−0.007 (0.01)	0.02 (0.01)*
Religiosity	0.27 (0.18)	0.26 (0.24)	−0.01 (0.23)
Education	0.20 (0.13)	0.18 (0.16)	0.03 (0.17)
Union membership	0.12 (0.41)	0.01 (0.52)	0.62 (0.48)
Type of neighbourhood	0.24 (0.19)	0.46 (0.26)	0.09 (0.25)
Partisanship incumbent	−3.58 (0.54)***	−2.94 (0.87)**	−2.75 (0.63)***
Privatization	0.09 (0.06)	0.09 (0.08)	−0.14 (0.10)
Pensions individual responsibility	0.06 (0.05)	0.04 (0.07)	−0.06 (0.09)
Growth (vs. protection of environment)	−0.04 (0.05)	−0.09 (0.07)	−0.03 (0.07)
Law and order (vs. civic freedoms)	0.03 (0.05)	0.14 (0.05)*	−0.12 (0.06)*
Abortion illegal (vs. legal)	0.13 (0.04)**	0.12 (0.05)*	−0.10 (0.06)
Retrospective personal economy	0.18 (0.18)	−0.03 (0.24)	−0.29 (0.24)
Retrospective national economy	−0.30 (0.15)*	−0.39 (0.22)	−.11 (0.20)
Government performance	−1.59 (0.29)***	−1.58 (0.40)***	−1.83 (0.35)***
Intercept	0.19 (1.36)	0.34 (1.67)	4.89 (1.58)**
N		609	
Pseudo R-squared (McFadden)		0.35	

Notes: *p<0.5; **p<0.01; ***p<0.001. Robust standard errors in parentheses.

Table A3. Multinomial logit analysis of the vote in the 2011 elections in Portugal. PS (main incumbent party) as the reference category

	PSD	CDS-PP	CDU
Female	−1.16 (0.39)**	−1.50 (0.57)**	−1.39 (0.50)**
Age	−0.002 (0.01)	−0.03 (0.02)	−0.002 (0.02)
Religiosity	0.61 (0.24)*	0.40 (0.43)	−0.29 (0.30)
Education	0.20 (0.17)	0.41 (0.22)	−0.08 (0.22)
Union membership	−0.42 (0.58)	−0.37 (0.76)	1.19 (0.56)*
Type of neighbourhood	0.63 (0.28)*	0.53 (0.39)	0.75 (0.34)*
Partisanship incumbent	−2.79 (0.48)***	−1.69 (0.47)***	−3.98 (1.03)***
Privatization	−0.12 (0.11)	−0.13 (0.16)	−0.08 (0.13)
Pensions individual responsibility	0.08 (0.07)	0.08 (0.11)	0.05 (0.09)
Growth (vs. protection of environment)	−0.09 (0.09)	0.005 (0.14)	0.07 (0.10)
Law and order (vs. civic freedoms)	0.18 (0.09)*	0.17 (0.13)	0.04 (0.10)
Abortion illegal (vs. legal)	0.15 (0.06)*	0.15 (0.10)	0.07 (0.08)
Retrospective personal economy	−0.13 (0.26)	0.16 (0.49)	−0.62 (0.38)
Retrospective national economy	−0.06 (0.24)	−0.55 (0.80)	−0.91 (0.38)*
Government performance	−2.62 (0.51)***	−2.26 (0.63)***	−1.42 (0.72)*
Intercept	3.51 (2.08)	2.77 (2.50)	
N		415	
Pseudo R-squared (McFadden)		0.36	

Notes: *p<0.5; **p<0.01; ***p<0.001. Robust standard errors in parentheses.

Table A4. Multinomial logit analysis of the vote in the 2011 elections in Portugal. PS (main incumbent party) as the reference category

	PSD	CDS-PP	CDU
Female	−1.06 (0.42)*	−1.44 (0.68)*	−1.19 (0.54)*
Age	−0.01 (0.01)	−0.04 (0.02)	−0.01 (0.02)
Religiosity	0.84 (0.25)**	0.71 (0.41)	0.01 (0.31)
Education	0.22 (0.18)	0.47 (0.27)	0.02 (0.24)
Union membership	−0.20 (0.62)	−0.21 (1.01)	1.39 (0.68)*
Type of neighbourhood	0.49 (0.26)	0.27 (0.47)	0.49 (0.35)
Partisanship incumbent	−2.49 (0.37)***	−1.73 (0.61)**	−3.93 (1.08)***
Privatization	0.02 (0.11)	0.04 (0.18)	0.00 (0.14)
Pensions individual responsibility	0.01 (0.08)	0.04 (0.13)	−0.01 (0.11)
Growth (vs. protection of environment)	0.02 (0.09)	0.09 (0.15)	0.13 (0.12)
Law and order (vs. civic freedoms)	0.18 (0.09)*	0.21 (0.15)	0.07 (0.11)
Abortion illegal (vs. legal)	0.17 (0.07)*	0.14 (0.12)	0.07 (0.09)
Retrospective personal economy	−0.06 (0.29)	0.23 (0.49)	−0.51 (0.38)
Retrospective national economy	−1.93 (0.08)	−4.91 (1.83)**	−3.28 (1.58)*
Government performance	−2.52 (0.47)***	−2.38 (0.72)**	−1.51 (0.60)*
Government exclusive responsibility	0.44 (0.18)*	0.02 (0.29)	−0.01 (0.24)
EU responsibility	−1.06 (0.54)*	−2.30 (0.77)**	−1.26 (0.70)
EU responsibility*Retrospective economy	0.53 (0.32)	1.30 (0.51)*	0.69 (0.46)
Intercept	6.17 (2.90)*	8.21 (4.23)	8.48 (3.58)*
N		403	
Pseudo R-squared (McFadden)		0.40	

Notes: *p<0.5; **p<0.01; ***p<0.001. Robust standard errors in parentheses.

The Incumbent Electoral Defeat in the 2011 Spanish National Elections: The Effect of the Economic Crisis in an Ideological Polarized Party System

MARIANO TORCAL
Universitat Pompeu Fabra, Spain

ABSTRACT   *This article examines the effect of the economic crisis on voting preferences in the 2011 Spanish national election. Specifically we demonstrate that Spanish voters' reactions to the economic crisis were not uniform and that their evaluations of the economic situation and final electoral decisions were conditioned by prior ideological preferences. Our findings have several important consequences for the economic voting model. First, in a more polarized party system how voters evaluate the economic performance of the incumbent is a better predictor of vote choice than evaluations of the economy as a whole. Second, this effect varies depending on where parties are located and competing ideologically. Finally, those effects are more conditional on voters' ideological predispositions than the effects of voters' evaluations of the situation of the economy.*

Since 2008 Spain has experienced one of the most severe economic crises in its recent history. This crisis began and reached its full intensity during the period of the last Socialist government (2008–2011). At the end of this period, the incumbent party, the *Partido Socialista Obrero Español* (PSOE) suffered its largest electoral defeat ever while the major opposition party, the conservative *Partido Popular* (PP) increased its share of the vote, as did several small state-wide parties such as the left-wing *Izquierda Unida* (IU) party and the new centrist party, the *Unión Progreso y Democracia* (UPyD). This article focuses on the electoral consequences of the Spanish economic crisis on vote choices in the 2011 general election. In what way were the two occurrences – the economic crisis and the fragmentation of the party system – related? More specifically, to what extent was the electoral defeat of the

This article makes reference to supplementary material available on the publisher's website at http://dx.doi.org/10.1080/17457289.2014.891598

incumbent Socialists due to voters making negative retrospective evaluations of the economic situation?

Given the severity and timing of the economic crisis and the presence of an easily identifiable incumbent – the PSOE – that could be held to account it is evident that the Spanish 2011 national election provides an ideal context to test the economic voting theory, particularly in its retrospective form. According to this well established model of voting behaviour, individuals cast their vote based in large part on an assessment of how the economy has performed since the last election (Nadeau & Lewis-Beck, 2001).[1] Certainly at first glance the evidence strongly suggests that the Socialist electoral defeat was due to changes in voters' evaluations of the Spanish economy during the same time period.

As well as providing a new empirical test of economic voting this article seeks to expand the theoretical core of the model for understanding electoral outcomes during a period of significant economic crisis. Economic accountability does not happen in a vacuum. It occurs within the wider context of the party system, the spread of ideological competition and voters' existing preferences. A number of studies have shown how these context-related effects and particularly voters' ideological positions exert a significant filtering or "screening effect" on economic voting (Pattie & Johnston, 2001), leading to an under-estimation of effects of retrospective economic evaluations on voting (Fraile & Lewis-Beck, 2010; Lewis-Beck, 2006; Lewis-Beck et al., 2008). In this article we proceed from the starting point that economic performance evaluations interact with voters' ideological preferences. We extend this argument to make the claim that these screening effects occur to varying degrees across the ideological spectrum and that their impact depends on the existing areas of party competition and intensity of the conflict taking place within those areas.

The results of our analysis carry three key and inter-related messages for the theory of economic voting. The first is that the impact of retrospective economic evaluations is concentrated in particular areas of party competition. In the case of Spain, those voters who are located in the ideological centre where there is a greater voting 'elasticity' or a higher probability of changing party preferences are most likely to be influenced by economic evaluations when it comes to making voting decisions (Martínez Pérez, 2007). A second and related rather simple point is that all things being equal voters' evaluation of the incumbent party's performance has a greater impact on their vote choice than the more generic sociotropic evaluations of the economy. This is because economic prosperity or decline is a valence issue (Stokes, 1963: 373; Vavreck, 2009: 22), and thus the argument about the effect of the economic crisis hinges on which party should be credited or blamed for it (Lewis-Beck & Stegmaier, 2007: 530). This decision will, however, itself be influenced by voters' prior ideological position. The final point which follows as a direct consequence of the previous finding is that if ideological outlook or left–right placement does play a 'screening' role in determining economic voting, it does so through evaluations of the incumbent party's job in managing the economy.

To make our case this article is divided into three main sections. First we describe the key changes in party preferences among the voters who supported the Socialist party in

2008 in the Spanish elections of 2011. We then conduct two different analyses of economic voting in these elections that test the arguments presented above. Both analyses use data from a panel data set.[2] The first applies a multilevel model (with random intercepts) to the pre-election survey data to explain the variation in or "between" individuals' vote preferences. The second makes use of the panel structure and applies a longitudinal regression model to explain changes in vote choice over time.

The Theoretical Argument

As Pattie and Johnston have asserted (2001: 374), some of the early works on voting behaviour treated voters as homogenous in their reaction to economic situations and economic evaluations. This clearly holds true for initial academic study on the specific question of the effect of economic performance on voting preferences (Alvarez & Nagler, 1998; Ferejohn, 1986; Haller & Norpoth, 1994; Markus, 1992), and on individual-level research on economic voting (Kinder & Kiewiet, 1979, 1981; Mackuen et al., 1992; Nannestad & Paldam, 1994; Norpoth, 1996). However, an increasing number of scholars during the last two decades have pointed to the heterogeneity of economic voting behaviour and the moderating effects of various factors such as social group interaction (Linn & Nagler, 2005; Mutz & Mondak, 1997), levels of political knowledge and education (Mutz & Mondak, 1997; Pattie & Johnston, 2001) and also wider institutional structures (Anderson, 2000; Duch, 2001; Lewis-Beck, 1988; Nadeau et al., 2002; Norpoth, 2001; Powell & Whitten, 1993; Rudolph, 2003; Whitten & Palmer, 1999).

A number of studies have extended this line of reasoning to individuals' ideological views and party attachments and argued they are likely to condition their evaluations of the economy and thus the extent to which a voter will exert sanctions on an incumbent. This so-called "screening effect" (Conover et al., 1987) is seen as operating largely through the left–right scale in Europe (Lewis-Beck & Nadeau, 2000; Nadeau et al., 2002; Pattie & Johnston, 2001; Anderson et al., 2004; Evans & Anderson, 2006; Fraile & Lewis-Beck, 2010, 2014; Lewis-Beck, 2006; Lewis-Beck et al., 2008). Efforts to contain the endogeneity problems that occur through instrumental variables have actually shown the effect of economic evaluations increases once the effect of these prior political attitudes is applied. Despite the growing evidence of the existence of these screening effects, our understanding of exactly how they work remains quite limited. Party identification or ideological preferences are often used as "running tallies" or proxies for economic evaluations in voting models (Linn et al., 2010: 16–18) rather than active and powerful filters as the hypothesis would suggest.

In this article we seek to develop a clearer theoretical and empirical understanding of the screening role of these attitudes within economic voting models. Following Bartels (2002) we argue that these orientations constitute "a pervasive dynamic force that shapes citizens' perceptions of, and reactions to, the political world" (Bartels, 2002: 138). Ideological preferences serve as filters or lenses that generate different readings of the same "reality" for different voters. From the perspective of economic voting this means that an individual's existing ideological preferences can moderate their perception of the magnitude of an economic decline or crisis and its consequences. This may substantially diminish the perceived negative effects of the economic crisis and thus the propensity for attribution of responsibility. In other words these attitudes help to "anchor" the vote and reduce the amount of switching or electoral elasticity that occurs in an election. Furthermore, given that it is through this switching that much of the economic punishment of the incumbent takes place (Brug et al., 2007), we hypothesise that partisanship and ideological outlook actually serve to decrease the amount of economic voting that takes place in a given election. This anchoring effect we argue is particularly strong for the left–right scale in Europe and it is this variable that forms the focus for our analysis of the screening hypothesis.

The choice of left–right placement over partisanship in the Spanish case is justified on a number of grounds. First, the left–right dimension is generally regarded as the primary axis of party competition in Europe (Aldrich et al., 2010: 5) and the main mechanism through which voters choose a party to represent them (Blais et al., 2004; Freire, 2006; Mair, 2007).[3] While partisanship is recognized as relevant it is generally seen as a less useful cue for voters than other information short-cuts available to them (Downs, 1957; Shively, 1979). In addition, from a methodological standpoint, party identification in Europe is quite highly correlated with the vote itself (Thomassen & Rosema, 2009), which makes any attempt to deal with the endogeneity issues and separate out a "pure screening effect" of partisanship on the vote even more difficult than it would otherwise be.

In examining the extent to which ideological preferences affect the impact of economic evaluations on the vote it is clear that this can occur in different ways depending on the wider political context. A key factor to consider first is the extent of ideological division with a party system. The classic "economic sanctioning model" (Duch & Stevenson, 2008: 10) contends that individuals vote against the incumbents based upon purely negative retrospective sociotropic evaluations of the economic situation (Bartels, 2011; Brug et al., 2007; Kiewiet & Rivers, 1984; Kinder & Kiewiet, 1979, 1981; Lewis-Beck, 1988; Markus, 1992; Sanders, 1996). However, recent work has argued that economic prosperity is more of a "valence" than a "positional" issue (Vavreck, 2009), meaning that its effect on voters is not based on their assessment of the general economic situation but on parties' and leaders' records in managing the economy and their policy proposals (Fiorina, 1981; Stokes, 1963, 1992). If this is the case then where party systems are more polarized we would expect evaluations of incumbent economic performance to matter more than retrospective economic evaluations given that those evaluations are more strongly related to ideological predispositions (Duch & Stevenson, 2008: 12–13).[4] During an economic crisis questions of competence and accountability are likely to be further heightened, making the economy even more of a valence issue (Clarke et al., 2009) and thus susceptible to the influence of ideological preferences.

As well as the extent of ideological polarization at the system level making a difference we would also expect the screening effect to vary among individuals depending on their location on the ideological spectrum. Voters located in different areas of party competition will have different degrees of ideological anchoring which will condition their desire to punish the incumbent party for an economic crisis.[5] In particular we contend that economic voting will be more prevalent among those citizens located at the ideological centre who have a more neutral and independent outlook (Duch et al., 2000; Mackuen & Mouw, 1995; Stokes, 1996) and thus are less intense and anchored to their vote choice, as the directional theory of voting predicts (MacDonald et al., 1991; Orriols & Balcells, 2012; Rabinowitz & MacDonald, 1989). The ideological centre (position 5 on the scale) in Spain conforms to these expectations. As well as being the place where voters most frequently locate themselves, those that do locate themselves here show the greatest propensity to change party preferences and display the greatest issue-content ambiguity (Calle & Roussias, 2012; Queralt, 2012; Torcal, 2011).

Based on the preceding discussion we set out four interconnected hypotheses concerning how economic voting takes place in more ideologically divided party systems:

H1: If economic voting occurs then it is most likely to take place through an evaluation of the governing party's performance rather than sociotropic evaluations of the state of the economy as a whole.

H2: Economic voting will be most evident among voters located at the ideological centre of party competition (i.e. in Spain between those voting for the PSOE/PP and PSOE/UPyD).

H3: Ideological preferences work as "screening devices" (and not as simply "running tallies") which means they will moderate the impact of economic evaluations on vote choice.

H4: Those moderating effects will be more evident in evaluations of the incumbent party's performance than in pure sociotropic evaluations of the economy.

The Economic Crisis and the 2011 Spanish National Election

The Spanish financial crisis began in 2008 as part of the global economic crisis that first began in 2007 in the United States. The Spanish economy was one of the most severely affected by the international situation due to the high external deficit it had accumulated during the earlier economic boom, making it susceptible to changing macroeconomic and financial conditions. In particular, the country faced a correction of an overinflated real estate market. Housing investment, which exceeded 12% of GDP during the boom period suffered a heavy crash, dropping to less than 7% in 2011 (Ortega & Peñalosa, 2012: 24f.). The deterioration of the economy and rising unemployment put additional stress on the balance sheets of public finances and financial institutions that were already exposed to a greater real estate risk. Spain went into recession in the second quarter of 2008 and remained there until the beginning of 2010, when a modest recovery occurred. The recovery cooled off again in the second half of 2011 when the sovereign debt crisis worsened in a number of European countries (Ortega & Peñalosa, 2012: 7).

The Spanish financial and economic crisis between 2008 and 2011 was both swift and dramatic in its effects. In a short period of time the country saw a sharp rise in the unemployment rate[6] from 11.3% in 2008 to 21.6% in 2011. Public debt[7] showed an equally if even more dramatic rise, increasing by almost 70% between 2008 and 2011 to reach 736,468 million euro.[8] Although GDP had staged something of a recovery by 2011, inflation, as measured by consumer prices, increased by 5 points between 2008 and 2011 (see Appendix X for more detail on Spain's marcroeconomic performance during this time http://dx.doi.org/10.1080/17457289.2014.891598).

The economic turbulence was followed by some significant changes in the political situation. The Spanish elections held on 20 November 2011 resulted in heavy losses for the incumbent Socialist party (PSOE) and the return to power of the main conservative opposition party, the Partido Popular (PP). Unlike its previous victories in 1996 and 2000, however, the PP's majority was not obtained through the abstention of left-wing voters (Font & Mateos, 2007) but from the fragmentation and the defection of former PSOE voters to parties on both sides of the ideological spectrum.[9] Two smaller parties – the IU and the UPyD – did particularly well in that they both increased their vote share by over 3%, gaining just under 5% and just under 7% of the national vote respectively (see Appendix X for full details of the 2008 and 2011 election results http://dx.doi.org/10.1080/17457289.2014.891598).[10] The victory of PP was also helped by the electoral system which magnified its victory (Martín & Urquizu-Sancho, 2012).

This fragmentation of the left-wing's vote is also evident from survey data and party system metrics covering the two election periods. According to CIS post-election data the PSOE suffered the highest number of defections between 2008 and 2011, with only three-fifths of its voters remaining faithful across the two elections. The PP faced far less defection with a full 92% of its supporters remaining faithful. Defectors from the PSOE were split quite widely across the spectrum. Of the 40% that switched their vote, the largest share went to the PP (16%), followed by the IU (5%) and UPyD (4%) as well as various smaller parties (5%). The final 10% abstained from voting entirely. Overall the 2011 election saw the lowest levels of individual party loyalty – 52% – since 1982 (48%) and the highest levels of voter volatility across the same 30-year time period (Martín & Urquizu-Sancho, 2012). Finally the effective number of electoral parties (ENEP), which had fallen successively for over 20 years from 4.1 in 1989 to 2.8 in 2008 (Torcal & Lago, 2008), saw an upswing in 2011 to 3.4.

Despite the instability in voting patterns at the individual and aggregate level voters' perceptions of the ideological positions of the major parties remained remarkably constant. The average perceived position of the PSOE and PP on the scale during the last three decades was 4.3 and 7.4 respectively. According to the CIS 2011 pre- and post-electoral studies (using the same scale) the scores had changed only marginally to 4.1 and 7.9. The same stability can be observed with the progressive IU which was scaled at 2.6 during the preceding decades and then 2.4 in both 2011 electoral surveys. The UPyD has had a stable position around 5.0 since its establishment[11] and maintained it for the most recent 2011 election. Looking more closely at the ideological self-placement of the swinging voters it is clear that (with the exception of those that defected to the more left-wing IU) most PSOE voters that swung to other parties occupied the centre position (i.e. position 5). The highest percentage of demobilized PSOE voters were in position 4, these people largely preferred abstention over swinging to other parties (reproducing patterns from past elections) (Font & Mateos, 2007).

In answer to our starting question about the impact of the economic recession on the 2011 Spanish election, therefore, this initial review of the behavioural data is consistent with the idea that the incumbent party was punished over the economy and that this occurred primarily among its ideologically centrist voters and to a lesser extent among its more leftist voters. As such we can claim some provisional support to our hypotheses, particularly H1 and H2.

A preliminary analysis of the accompanying attitudinal data, however, raises some questions about the validity of this interpretation, at least in terms of PSOE voters' evaluations of the Spanish economic situation. The distribution of economic evaluations is equally negative (around 85–90%) among PSOE voters that remained loyal in 2011 and those that defected. This lack of variance is also found across all ideological positions. The story changes only marginally once retrospective economic evaluations are taking into account. Here we find that loyal PSOE voters were somewhat more likely to consider that the economic situation during the last four years has improved (8%) than those who defected to the PP (3%) or the UPyD (5%). To explore these findings further and more rigorously test our hypotheses we move to our multivariate analysis of the electoral study 2011 CIS panel data.

Estimating the Effects of Economic Evaluations on the 2011 Election

Given the increasing recognition of the screening or moderating impact of partisanship and ideology on economic voting there has been a growing use of panel data where possible to address the problems of endogeneity that arise (Linn et al., 2010: 16; see also Fraile & Lewis-Beck, 2010, 2014). Here we follow suit and carry out a longitudinal regression analysis using the Spanish electoral panel data for the 2011 elections. Given that the first wave of the panel took place only a few weeks before the elections the variation in party preferences between time t_{-1} and time t are likely to be very low. The rate of change in vote choice from the PSOE to PP and the IU reflects this with both standing at less than 4%. Thus, much of shift in voter preferences took place during the previous legislative term and before the electoral campaign started (Barreiro & Sánchez-Cuenca, 2012; Martín & Urquizu-Sancho, 2012).

This lack of variation in party choices between t_{-1} and t prompted two key methodological decisions in our analysis. First, propensity to vote (PTV) was used as the dependent variable instead of discrete-choice variables. The advantages of using PTV in modelling electoral behaviour have been widely discussed (Eijk et al., 2006).[12] A key benefit derived from its use in this analysis is that it significantly increases our N. Use of discrete-choice voting in t_{-1} substantially reduces the number of cases for analysis given that many respondents did not report or had not yet made up their minds about who they would vote for at that particular moment. PTV also displays a greater level of time variance between t_{-1} and t than the discrete-choice variables. Finally, because PSOE's losses went largely to small parties in the Spanish multi-party system, such as the IU and the UPyD, using PTV as the dependent variable produces clearer, unbiased and more efficient coefficients. In this case, three different dependent variables are created at the individual level measuring the differential propensities of voting for four different parties: propensity of voting for the PP minus the propensity of voting for the PSOE (PP-PSOE); propensity of voting for the IU minus the propensity of voting for the PSOE (IU-PSOE); and finally, propensity of voting for the UPyD minus the propensity of voting for the PSOE (UPyD-PSOE).[13]

The second key decision prompted by the lack of variation in party choice across the two time periods was that we supplemented our longitudinal analysis of change in the vote with a cross-sectional study of PTV at t_{-1} using a multilevel regression model with *random intercepts*. This model is suitable for purposes of this analysis due to the hierarchical nature of the data collected in the 17 Spanish regions. In addition, further tests on the data show that while we cannot assume voters' party-utilities or PTVs are comparable among individuals across Spain, we can assume a uniform effect of our two key independent variables on PTV.[14] Below we report the results for each model separately beginning with the hierarchical multilevel model with PTV differentials at t_{-1} as the dependent variable. We then move to the results of the longitudinal linear regression model with random effects estimating the effect of time variance economic evaluations (t_{-1} and t) on time-variance differential PTVs.

Step 1: A Multilevel Analysis of Variance in (between) Vote Choice in the 2011 Election

To fully evaluate the effect of the economic crisis on the observed PSOE electoral decline and test H1 we estimate a model with two types of economic attitudes as independent variables. The first is current evaluations of the situation of the economy and the second is the more particular evaluation of the PSOE's economic performance at the time of the pre-election survey. Both variables have the same five categories of response (very bad, bad, fair, good and very good) and display a similarly skewed distribution. Only 1.3% of Spaniards said in October 2011 that the current economic situation was "good" or "very good", and only 2.5% declared that the PSOE economic performance was "good" or "very good". While this limited variance is clearly problematic in that it reduces the likelihood that economic evaluations will be found to be significant in predicting voting behaviour (Fraile & Lewis-Beck, 2014), the fact that it applies to both independent variables to a similar degree is helpful in so far as it standardizes the problem across the two predictors.

To test our four hypotheses we run a series of three models to predict each of our three dependent variables. The first (M1) only contains two variables: current evaluation of the state of the economy and evaluation of the PSOE's economic performance. The second (M2), includes these same variables, along with the respondent's self-placement on an ideological scale (1 to 10), as well as its interaction with current evaluations of the state of the economy. Finally, the third model (M3) substitutes the former interaction term with the one between ideology and the PSOE's economic performance evaluation. These additional variables allow us to test H2, H3 and H4 in addition to H1. To provide a better understanding of the interactive terms of the equation, both variables are transformed into dummy variables. The results are robust and correspond very closely to the findings using the original variables.[15] In the second and third models (M2 and M3) we add controls for socio-demographic factors that predict party choice in Spain (Montero & Lago, 2010; Montero et al., 2007), and a range of standard controls used in economic voting models in general (Duch & Stevenson, 2008: 47) and in Spain more particularly (Fraile & Lewis-Beck, 2014).

The results of the estimation of these models are displayed in Table 1. The table shows that the coefficients for both evaluation variables are significant and in the expected direction in all three models confirming that economic issues were important in determining voter preferences in the lead up to the election.

More importantly, however, the results show that evaluations of the performance of the PSOE in managing the economy were a more important predictor of the differential propensity to vote in all three models than general evaluations of the state of the economy, thereby confirming H1. Furthermore, the economic accountability model works better in reference to parties that compete for voters at the centre of the ideological spectrum (PP-PSOE and UPyD-PSOE) than parties that do so for voters at the left of the ideological spectrum (PSOE-IU), confirming H2. The goodness of the fit improves substantially (Wald Chi^2) and coefficients are larger in these cases. The results of M2 and M3 are very interesting in that we find a significant interaction effect in predicting party preferences between evaluations of the PSOE's economic performance and ideological self-placement (except for the competition PSOE/PP), confirming the screening effect of pre-existing ideological predispositions on the effect of economic variables on party preferences (H3). However, the interaction term between the ideological scale and voters' sociotropic evaluations of the current economic situation is not only smaller but also non-significant for all three models (PSOE/PP, PSOE/IU and PSOE/UPyD). This confirms that the evaluation of the PSOE's economic performance is the most relevant variable in predicting the outcome and that its effects are conditioned by pre-existing ideological positions (H4).

To provide a more intuitive interpretation of the interactions, the marginal effects of the PSOE's economic performance evaluation on each of the dependent variables are calculated, conditional on where a respondent places themselves on the left–right scale (Figures 1, 2 and 3). The results show that the marginal effect of party incumbent economic performance is significant for all three models that include this interactive term but that this does not apply evenly across the ideological spectrum. The marginal effects of a negative evaluation of the incumbent's economic performance on the probability of voting for the PSOE are consistently found among voters

Table 1. Multilevel regression analysis of the probability of voting for the PSOE versus parties of the opposition (maximum likelihood estimators)

	Probability of supporting PP-PSOE			Probability of supporting IU-PSOE			Probability of supporting UPyD-PSOE		
	M1	M2	M3	M1	M2	M3	M1	M2	M3
Economic evaluation	−1.59*** (0.29)	−1.31** (0.54)	−1.29*** (0.26)	−0.82*** (0.18)	−1.12*** (0.38)	−0.68*** (0.18)	−1.20*** (0.20)	−1.47*** (0.41)	−0.95*** (0.19)
PSOE economic performance evaluation	−5.62*** (0.21)	−4.44*** (0.20)	−4.66*** (0.40)	−2.67*** (0.14)	−2.50*** (0.14)	−3.02*** (0.28)	−3.50*** (0.15)	−2.98*** (0.15)	−3.69*** (0.30)
Ideological self-placement		1.02*** (0.03)	1.01*** (0.03)		0.11*** (0.02)	0.10*** (0.02)		0.42*** (0.02)	0.41*** (0.02)
Ideological self-placement *Economic evaluation		0.00 (0.09)			0.09 (0.07)			0.11 (0.07)	
Ideological self-placement *PSOE economic performance evaluation			0.04 (0.07)			0.11** (0.05)			0.15*** (0.06)
Control variables (age, education, class, gender)	NI	Included	Included	NI	Included	Included	NI	Included	Included
Intercept	1.92*** (0.23)	−4.90*** (0.44)	−4.86*** (0.04)	−1.14*** (0.11)	−1.63*** (0.29)	−1.58*** (0.29)	−1.13*** (0.18)	−3.98*** (0.33)	−3.90*** (0.33)
Random effects									
Variance of the intercept	0.86 (0.18)	0.71 (0.16)	0.71 (0.16)	0.38 (0.09)	0.30 (0.09)	0.29 (0.09)	0.69 (0.14)	0.59 (0.12)	0.59 (0.12)
Wald Chi²	867.0***	2331.3***	2331.8***	500.0***	680.7***	683.7***	713.7***	1280.2***	1286.5***
N	5,336	5,158	5,158	5,222	5,047	5,047	4,911	4,748	4,748
Groups	17	17	17	17	17	17	17	17	17

Notes: * $p<0.1$, ** $p<0.05$, *** $p<0.01$.
Source: Centro de Investigaciones Sociológicas, Electoral Study 2011.

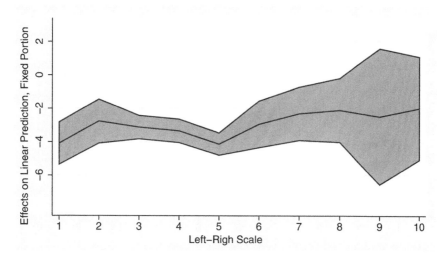

Figure 1. Average Marginal Effects of PSOE Economic Performance Evaluation by ideology on the PSOE/PP competition.
Source: Centro de Investigaciones Sociológicas, Electoral Study 2011

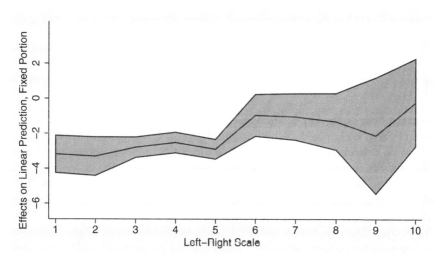

Figure 2. Average Marginal Effects of PSOE Economic Performance Evaluation by ideology on the PSOE/UPyD competition.
Source: Centro de Investigaciones Sociológicas, Electoral Study 2011

placing themselves on the left and centre when voters are choosing between the PSOE-IU and PSOE-UPyD. Marginal effects of the PSOE's government economic performance on voting preferences are not significant in discriminating vote choice

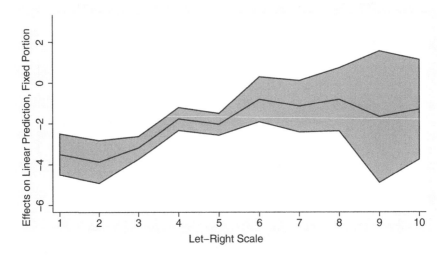

Figure 3. Average Marginal Effects of PSOE Economic Performance Evaluation by ideology on the PSOE/IU competition.
Source: Centro de Investigaciones Sociológicas, Electoral Study 2011

among voters placing themselves on the right side of the scale; i.e. those who would be most inclined to support the PP.

Step 2: A Longitudinal Analysis of Variance (within) Individual Vote Choice in the 2011 Election

Given that both of our key independent variables – individuals' subjective assessments of the economy and of the incumbent party's economic performance – are likely to be determined to a degree by their ideological predispositions this section of the analysis re-tests the hypotheses with controls to reduce the endogeneity that is expected to be present. To do so we exploit the panel data aspect of the 2011 CIS study which measured vote intention one a month before the election occurred (t_{-1}), and again immediately after the election (t). This structure of the data allows us to estimate time variance-component models and test whether changes in individuals' views of the economy during the campaign had any effect on within individual variance on the dependent variable – the PTV differential between the incumbent PSOE and the other parties which received the majority of its lost votes.

The variables used in these longitudinal models are the same as before with only one difference, there is no 't' (i.e. second wave) measurement of the PSOE economic performance evaluation. Instead we use PSOE leader evaluation as a proxy (on a 1 to 10 point scale). In the first wave (i.e. time t_{-1}) the correlation between these two variables is 0.45. Before reporting the results it is important to note that despite the low voting transfers reported above we do see a considerable degree of variation in evaluations of the economy with these data. For our two key independent variables we find that the level of within individual (time variance) change in sociotropic evaluations of the *current* economic situation ran as high as 44% between the two time points. The PSOE leadership evaluation variable (our proxy measure of the PSOE's economic performance) displays even more time variance (64%). What we seek to explore next, therefore, is how far variation in these economic attitudes explain time change in PTVs?

To answer this question we estimate three longitudinal linear models with random effects (M1, M2 and M3) using the following three time variant independent variables: (1) the current sociotropic evaluation of the state of the economy; (2) the PSOE leadership evaluation, as a proxy for PSOE's (economic) performance evaluation; (3) left/right self-placement; and (4) the interactions of variables 1 and 2 with the left–right scale. The results of our analysis are presented in Table 2.

The findings show that in line with H1, the PSOE leadership evaluation measure (our proxy for PSOE economic management) is more important in predicting time PTV differential transfers than sociotropic evaluations of the economic situation in all M1 models. Furthermore the significance of sociotropic evaluations is removed once ideology added to the models (M2) whereas PSOE's leadership remain significant and robust. If we compare the coefficients across all models it is clear that evaluations of PSOE's leadership have a greater effect on the transfers between PP-PSOE and UPyD-PSOE (i.e. those occurring at the centre of the ideological spectrum) than those taking place between the PSOE and the more leftist IU. This supports H2 in that it indicates that evaluations of the PSOE economic performance had a stronger influence on less ideologically anchored voters. Finally, the only interaction term which is (again) significant in predicting voting preferences (PTV change between t-1 and t) is that between the evaluation of PSOE's leadership and left–right placement. This is true for for all three dependent variables (PSOE-PP; PSOE-IU; PSOE-UPyD) and follows a similar pattern to that shown in preceding analysis in being negative and becoming weaker as an individual moves further to the right of the scale. These results thus provide further support for H3 and H4.

Final Discussion

In terms of the original question posed here – was the incumbent party (the PSOE) punished in 2011 for its handling of the economic crisis – our results strongly confirm this. However in addition to this broad conclusion we have also shown how this punishment is conditioned by prior ideological attachments. Essentially the perceived effects of the economic crisis were not uniform across voters. Dissatisfaction with the incumbent's performance and punishment based on that dissatisfaction was meted out largely by centrist former voters for the PSOE who switched to support either to smaller parties on the centre-right or to the PP itself. These findings are significant in that they expand on those of Fraile who demonstrated impact of the economy on Spanish citizens' vote choice is conditioned by issue prevalence during the election (Fraile, 2005, 2007). Here we show how other more deep-seated political

Table 2. Longitudinal analysis of vote preference change during the electoral campaign (random effects) (maximum likelihood estimators)

	Probability of supporting PP-PSOE			Probability of supporting IU-PSOE			Probability of supporting UPyD-PSOE		
	M1	M2	M3	M1	M2	M3	M1	M2	M3
Change in economic evaluation	-0.19**	-0.24	-0.15	-0.16**	-0.09	-0.01	-0.19**	-0.24	-0.17
	(0.08)	(0.16)	(0.16)	(0.07)	(0.14)	(0.14)	(0.08)	(0.15)	(0.16)
Change in evaluation of PSOE leadership	-0.43***	-0.40***	-0.56***	-0.27***	-0.27***	-0.42***	-0.30***	-0.29***	-0.44***
	(0.03)	(0.03)	(0.05)	(0.03)	(0.02)	(0.05)	(0.03)	(0.03)	(0.05)
Change in ideological self-placement		0.24***	0.14**		0.02	-0.07		0.05	-0.05
		(0.05)	(0.06)		(0.04)	(0.05)		(0.05)	(0.05)
Change in economic evaluation *Change in ideological self-placement		0.01	-0.01		-0.01	-0.03		0.01	-0.004
		(0.03)	(0.03)		(0.02)	(0.02)		(0.03)	(0.03)
Change in evaluation of PSOE leadership *Change in ideological self-placement		Ni	0.03***		Ni	0.03***		Ni	0.03***
			(0.008)			(0.007)			(0.007)
Constant	2.57***	1.17***	1.81***	-0.19	0.32	0.31	-0.21	-0.51*	0.12
	(0.19)	(0.32)	(0.36)	(0.16)	(0.28)	(0.32)	(0.17)	(0.31)	(0.35)
R-squared within	0.05	0.08	0.08	0.03	0.03	0.03	0.04	0.04	0.04
R-squared between	0.41	0.52	0.52	0.23	0.23	0.25	0.37	0.38	0.40
R-squared overall	0.37	0.47	0.47	0.19	0.18	0.20	0.31	0.33	0.34
Rho	0.77	0.76	0.76	0.63	0.63	0.62	0.66	0.66	0.66
Number of groups	2	2	2	2	2	2	2	2	2
N	10,005	10,005	10,005	9,784	9,784	9,784	9,116	9,116	9,116

Notes: * $p<0.1$, ** $p<0.05$, *** $p<0.01$.
Source: Centro de Investigaciones Sociológicas, Electoral Study 2011.

attitudes and values shape and moderate that relationship. Our results also make clear the extent of the fragmentation the Spanish party system experienced following the election of 2011. Essentially the PP's majority was illusory in that it did not occur through the transfers of the vote from the PSOE but from the combination of the majoritarian bias in the system and the fragmentation of the PSOE vote around the left and centre-left.

The findings of this analysis of the 2011 Spanish elections also carry some important implications for the economic voting literature. First, we have shown that while economic evaluations do affect voters' likelihood of supporting the incumbent party, in those countries with a more ideologically divided electorate, evaluations of the overall state of the economy have weaker effects on defection from the incumbent party than evaluations of the incumbent party's performance. Second, the existing party supply and extent of voters' ideological anchoring diminishes their "propensity to swing" (or the amount of electoral elasticity occurring in a given election) to a significant degree, thereby confining the electoral economic accountability mechanism to particular areas of party competition. The classical economic performance sanctioning model applies largely to the more "relaxed" ideological areas of party competition where more retrospective voters are concentrated. Finally, we find a stronger significant interactive effect on voting preferences between ideological predispositions and evaluations of the incumbent party's economic performance. This finding suggests that voters' predispositions are not simply the "running tallies" of performance evaluations that appears to be the "default" position of the existing literature. Instead it reveals further support for the idea that voters use ideological preferences as an informational short-cut to evaluate party incumbent economic performance (Pattie & Johnston, 2001). This is clearly a question that deserves further research in the future.

Funding Statement

The work of this article has been made possible with the funding of the Spanish Ministry of Innovation and Science, research project reference: CSO2009-14434.

Notes

1. Prospective economic voting occurs only when there is no clear incumbent to blame for the economic crisis (Linn et al., 2010: 9). It is less common since it generally requires more cognitive effort by voters (Fiorina, 1981: 10). Other studies using economic voting models include that of Kramer (1983) Powell and Whitten (1993), Anderson (1995, 2000), Whitten and Palmer (1999), Nadeu and Lewis-Beck (2001) and Duch and Stevenson (2008).
2. The *Centro de Investigaciones Sociológicas* (CIS) has designed and applied a pre/post panel survey (studies 2,915 and 2,920) with a national representative sample of 6,200 respondents. To get the data set go to <www.cis.es>.
3. This is not to discount the well-documented criticisms that have been raised about the left–right self-placement scale on dimensionality, validity and reliability grounds (Johnston & Pattie, 2000, 2002; Kroh, 2010; Zechmeister, 2006). However, our goal here is not to identify what is the most valid

and empirically useful measure of this vote anchoring or screening effect in Spain from the alternatives available to us.

4. For the same argument in the British General election of 2007, see Clarke et al. (2009); and in the Portuguese General election of 2011, Magalhães (2012).

5. It could be argued that the limited voting elasticity produced by economic evaluations is also a problem of endogeneity between the latter and ideological preferences. I think that this argument is misleading; as the lack of economic voting elasticity should instead be attributed to the endogeneity between party preference and economic evaluations (Eijk et al., 2007), but this is a topic that cannot be addressed here.

6. Measured as the percentage of the active population above 15 years of age.

7. Here measured as General Government Debt according to the excessive deficit procedure. This includes the debt of the Central Government, Regional Governments and Local Governments.

8. Source: Banco de España (2012) Liabilities outstanding and debt according to the excessive deficit procedure. Absolute values. Available at <www.bde.es/webbde/es/estadis/infoest/a1103e.pdf> (accessed 13 November 2012).

9. The overall vote share of the two main parties dropped from 84% in 2008 to 73% in 2011 (Martín & Urquizu-Sancho, 2012: 347).

10. These trends had been emerging in the second-order elections that occurred in Spain during 2008–2011, 2009 European elections (Torcal & Font, 2012), the 2010 Catalan elections (Rico, 2012) and the most recent regional and local elections that took place in May 2011 (Barreiro & Sánchez Cuenca, 2012).

11. For these data on party ideological positions see CIS time-series indicators, <www.cis.es/cis/export/sites/default/-Archivos/Indicadores/documentos_html>.

12. The concepts of "party support" or "propensity to support a party" are equivalent to what Downs (1957) called "the utility for voting for a party" and constitute the first step in a model of electoral choice, with voting as the second step (Eijk et al., 2006: 426). For a further and recent discussion of this see Brug et al. (2007: 8–15).

13. This way we have a dependent variable that varies from -10 when the interviewee expresses a 10 on the probability of voting for the PSOE and a 0 on the probability of voting for the opposition party, to a score of +10 when the interviewee declares a 0 probability of voting for the PSOE and 10 on the probability of voting for the opposition party.

14. The Likelihood-Ratio (LR) test (not shown) suggests that the random intercepts should be kept. We cannot say the same for the random slopes of the relevant variables, which show that the effects of the evaluations of the current economic situation and of PSOE's economic performance evaluation are uniform across Spain, regardless of the economic situation in each of Spain's 17 regions. We have also tried to test if economic contextual variables explain the intercept variance or the retrospective economic evaluation slope variance by including in the model the following four macroeconomic indicators by region in Spain: unemployment increases between 2008 and 2011 in absolute numbers; public debt increases between 2008 and 2011 in absolute figures; GDP per capita decreases between 2008 and 2011; inflation rate changes between 2008 and 2011. All the coefficients were non-significant.

15. In both variables I have recoded categories "very bad" and "bad" as 0, and categories "neither good or bad", "good" and "very good" as 1.

References

Aldrich, J., Dorobantu, S. & Férnandez, M. Antonio (2010) The use of the left-right scale in individual's voting decisions. Annual meeting of the American Political Science Association, Washington.

Alvarez, R.M. & Nagler, J. (1998) Economics, entitlements, and social issues: voter choice in the 1996 presidential election. *American Journal of Political Science*, 42, pp. 1349–1363.

Anderson, C. (1995) *Blaming the Government: Citizens and the Economy in Five European Democracies* (London: M.E. Sharpe).

Anderson, C. (2000) Economic voting and political context: a comparative perspective. *Electoral Studies*, 19(2–3), pp. 151–170.

Anderson, C.J., Mendes, S.M. & Tverdova, Y.V. (2004) Endogenous economic voting: evidence from the 1997 British election. *Electoral Studies*, 23(4), pp. 683–708.

Barreiro, B. & Sánchez-Cuenca, I. (2012) In the whirlwind of the economic crisis: local and regional elections in Spain: the collapse of the socialist party. *Southern European Society and Politics*, 17(2), pp. 281–294.

Bartels, L.M. (2002) Beyong the running tally: partisan bias in political perceptions. *Political Behavior*, 24, pp. 117–150.

Bartels, L.M. (2011) Ideology and retrospection in electoral responses to the general recession. Paper presented at the conference on Popular Reactions to the Great Recession, Nuffield College, Oxford, 24–26 June.

Blais, A., Turgeon, M., Gidengil, E., Nevitte, N. & Nadeu, R. (2004) Which matters most? Comparing the impact of issues and the economy in American, British and Canadian elections. *British Journal of Political Science*, 34, pp. 555–564.

Brug, W. van der, Eijk, C. van der & Franklin, M. (2007) *The Economy and the Vote: Economic Conditions and Elections in Fifteen Countries* (Cambridge: Cambridge University Press).

Calle, de la L. & Roussias, N. (2012) How do Spanish independents vote? Ideology vs. performance. *Southern European Society and Politics*, 17(3), pp. 411–425.

Clarke, H.D., Sanders, D., Stewart, M. & Whiteley, P.F. (2009) *Performance Politics and the British Voters* (Cambridge: Cambridge University Press).

Conover, P., Feldman, S. & Knight, K. (1987) The personal and political underpinnings of economic forecasts. *American Journal of Political Science*, 31, pp. 559–583.

Downs, A. (1957) *An Economic Theory of Democracy* (New York: Harper & Row).

Duch, R.M. (2001) A developmental model of heterogeneous economic voting in new democracies. *American Political Science Review*, 95(4), pp. 895–910.

Duch, R. & Stevenson, R.T. (2008) *The Economic Vote: How Political and Economic Institutions Condition Election Results* (New York: Cambridge University Press).

Duch, R.M., Harvey, D.P. & Anderson C.J. (2000) Heterogeneity in perceptions of national economic conditions. *American Journal of Political Science*, 44(4), pp. 635–649.

Eijk, C. van der, Brug, W. van der, Kroh, M. & Franklin, M. (2006) Rethinking the dependent variable in voting behavior: on the measurement and analysis of electoral utilities. *Electoral Studies*, 25(3), pp. 424–447.

Eijk, C. van der, Franklin, M., Demant F. & Brug, W. van der (2007) The endogenous economy: "real" economic conditions, subjective economic evaluations and government support. *Acta Política*, 42(1), pp. 1–22.

Evans, G. & Anderson, C.J. (2006) The political conditioning of economic perceptions. *Journal of Politics*, 68(1), pp. 194–207.

Ferejohn, J. (1986) Incumbent performance and electoral control. *Public Choice*, 50(Fall), pp. 5–25.

Fiorina, M.P. (1981) Economic retrospective voting in American national elections: a micro-analysis. *American Journal of Political Science*, 22, pp. 426–443.

Font, J. & Mateos, A. (2007) La Participación Electoral, in: J.R. Montero, I. Lago & M. Torcal (eds) *Elecciones Generales 2004* (Madrid: Centro de Investigaciones Sociológicas), pp. 143–168.

Fraile, M. (2005) *Cuando la economía entra en urnas. El voto económico en España 1979–1996* (Madrid: Centro de Investigaciones Sociológicas).

Fraile, M. (2007) El Voto por Rendimientos: Los Temas Económicos y Sociales, in: J.R. Montero, I. Lago & M. Torcal (eds) *Elecciones Generales 2004* (Madrid: Centro de Investigaciones Sociológicas), pp. 205–223.

Fraile, M. & Lewis-Beck, M.S. (2010) Economic voting in Spain: a 2000 panel test. *Electoral Studies*, 29(2), pp. 210–220.

Fraile, M. & Lewis-Beck, M.S. (2014) Economic vote instability or restricted varience? Spanish panel evidence from 2008 and 2011. *European Journal of Political Research*, 53(1), pp. 160–179.

Freire, A. (2006) Party polarization and citizens' left-right orientations. *Party Politics*, 14(2), pp. 189–209.

Haller, H.B. & Norpoth, H. (1994) Let the good times roll: the economic expectations of U.S. voters. *American Journal of Political Science*, 38(3), pp. 625–650.

Johnston, R. & Pattie, C. (2000) Inconsistent individual attitudes within consistent attitudinal structures: comments on an important issue raised by John Bartle's paper on causal modelling in Britain. *British Journal of Political Science*, 30, pp. 697–698.

Johnston, R. & Pattie, C. (2002) Are inconsistent individual attitudes nothing more than random error? A response to Sturgis. *British Journal of Political Science*, 32, pp. 361–374.

Kiewiet, D.R. and Rivers, R.D. (1984) A retrospective on retrospective voting. *Political Behavior*, 6(4), pp. 1–26.

Kinder, D.R. & Kiewiet, D.R. (1979) Economic discontent and political behavior: the role of personal grievances and collective economic judgments in Congressional voting. *American Journal of Political Science*, 23, pp. 495–527.

Kinder, D.R. & Kiewiet, D.R. (1981) Sociotropic politics: the American case. *British Journal of Political Science*, 11, pp. 129–161.

Kramer, G.H. (1983) The ecological fallacy revisited: aggregate vs. individual-level findings on economics and elections, and sociotropic voting. *American Political Science Review*, 77(1), pp. 92–111.

Kroh, Martin (2010) Surveying the left-right dimension: the choice of response format. Working Paper, DIW Berlin.

Lewis-Beck, M.S. (1988) *Economic and Elections: The Major Western Democracies* (Ann Arbor: University of Michigan Press).

Lewis-Beck, M.S. (2006) Does economics still matters? Econometrics and the vote. *The Journal of Politics*, 68(1), pp. 208–212.

Lewis-Beck, M. & Nadeau, R. (2000) French electoral institutions and the economic vote. *Electoral Studies*, 19, pp. 171–182.

Lewis-Beck, M.S. & Stegmaier, M. (2007) Economic models of voting, in: R.J. Dalton & H.-D. Klingemann (eds) *The Oxford Handbook of Political Behavior* (Oxford: Oxford University Press), pp. 518–537.

Lewis-Beck, M.S., Nadeau, R. & Elias, R. (2008) Economics, party, and the vote: causality issues and panel data. *American Journal of Political Science*, 52(1), pp. 84–95.

Linn, S. & Nagler, J. (2005) Do voters really care who gets what? Economic growth, economic distribution, and presidential popularity. Paper presented at the Annual Meeting of the Midwest Political Science Association, Chicago.

Linn, S., Nagler, J. & Morales, M.A. (2010) Economics, elections and voting behavior, in: J.E. Leighley (ed.) *The Oxford Handbook of American Elections and Political Behavior* (Oxford: Oxford University Press), pp. 1–33.

MacDonald, S., Listhaug, O. & Rabinowitz, G. (1991) Issues and party support in multiparty systems. *American Political Science Review*, 85, pp. 1107–1132.

Mackuen, M.B. & Mouw, C. (1995) Class and competence in the political economy. Paper presented at the Conference on Economics and Political Behavior, Houston, Texas, 21–23 April.

Mackuen, M.B., Erickson, R.S. & Stimson, J.A. (1992) Peasants and bankers? The American electorate and the U.S. economy. *American Political Science Review*, 86, pp. 597–611.

Magalhães, P.C. (2012) After the bailout: responsibility, policy, and valence in the Portuguese legislative election of June 2011. *South European Society and Politics*, 17(2), pp. 309–327.

Mair, P. (2007) Left-right orientations, in: R.J. Dalton & H.-D. Klingemann (eds) *The Oxford Handbook of Political Behavior* (Oxford: Oxford University Press), pp. 206–222.

Markus, G.B. (1992) The impact of personal and national economic conditions on presidential voting, 1956–1988 (an update). *American Journal of Political Science*, 36, pp. 829–834.

Martín, I. & Urquizu-Sancho, I. (2012) The 2011 general election in Spain: the collapse of the socialist party. *Southern European Society and Politics*, 17(2), pp. 247–263.

Mártinez Pérez, A. (2007) Ideología, Gestión Gubernamental y Voto en las Elecciones Españolas, in: J.R. Montero, I. Lago & M. Torcal (eds) *Elecciones Generales 2004* (Madrid: Centro de Investigaciones Sociológicas), pp. 303–329.

Montero, J.R. & Lago, I. (2010) *Elecciones Generales 2008* (Madrid: Centro de Investigaciones Sociológicas).

Montero, J.R., Lago, I. & Torcal, M. (2007) *Elecciones Generales 2004* (Madrid: Centro de Investigaciones Sociológicas).

Mutz, D.C. & Mondak, J.J. (1997) Dimensions of sociotropic behavior: group-based judgments of fairness and well-being. *American Journal of Political Science*, 41(1), pp. 284–308.

Nadeau, R. & Lewis-Beck, M. (2001) National economic voting in U.S. presidential elections. *Journal of Politics*, 63(1), pp. 159–181.

Nadeau, R., Niemi, R.G. & Yoshinaka, A. (2002) A cross-national analysis of economic voting: taking account of the political context across time and nations. *Electoral Studies*, 21, pp. 403–423.

Nannestad, P. & Paldam, M. (1994) The VP-function: a survey of the literature on vote and popularity functions after 25 years. *Public Choice*, 79, pp. 213–245.

Norpoth, H. (1996) Presidents and the prospective voter. *Journal of Politics*, 58, pp. 776–792.

Norpoth, H. (2001) Divided government and economic voting. *Journal of Politics*, 63, pp. 414–435.

Orriols, Ll. & Balcells, L. (2012) Party polarization and spatial voting in Spain. *Southern European Society and Politics*, 17(3), pp. 343–409.

Ortega, E. & Peñalosa, J. (2012) The Spanish economic crisis: key factors and growth challenges in the Euro area (Madrid: Banco de España) Paper N° 1201.

Pattie, C.J. & Johnston, R.J. (2001) Routes to party choice: ideology, economic evaluations and voting at the 1997 British general election. *European Journal of Political Research*, 39, pp. 373–389.

Powell, G.B. & Whitten G.D. (1993) A cross-national analysis of economic voting: taking account of the political context. *American Journal of Political Science*, 37, pp. 391–414.

Queralt, D. (2012) Spatial voting in Spain. *South European Society and Politics*, 17(3), pp. 375–392.

Rabinowitz, G. & MacDonald, S. (1989) A directional theory of issue voting. *American Political Science Review*, 83, pp. 93–121.

Rico, G. (2012) The 2010 regional election in Catalonia: a multilevel account in an age of economic crisis. *Southern European Society and Politics*, 17(2), pp. 217–238.

Rudolph, T.J. (2003) Institutional context and the assignment of political responsibility. *Journal of Politics*, 65(1), pp. 190–215.

Sanders, D. (1996) Economic performance, management competence and the outcome of the next general election. *Political Studies*, 44, pp. 203–231.

Shively, P. (1979) The development of party identification among adults: explanation of functional model. *American Political Science Review*, 73, pp. 1039–1054.

Stokes, D.S. (1963) Spatial models of party competition. *The American Political Science Review*, 57(2), pp. 368–377.

Stokes, D.S. (1992) Valence politics, in: D. Kavanagh (ed.) *Electoral Politics* (Oxford: Claredon Press), pp. 141–162.

Stokes, S.C. (1996) Economic reform and public opinion in Peru 1990–1995. *Comparative Political Studies*, 29, pp. 544–566.

Thomassen, J. & Rosema, M. (2009) Party identification revisited, in: J. Bartle & P. Bellucci (eds) *Political Parties and Partisanship: Social Identity and Individual Attitudes* (London: Routledge/ECPR Series in European Political Science), pp. 42–59.

Torcal, M. (2011) El significado y el contenido del Centro Ideológico en España (Madrid: Fundación Alternativas) Working paper.

Torcal, M. & Font, J. (2012) *Elecciones Europeas 2009* (Madrid: Centro de Investigaciones Sociológicas).

Torcal, M. & Lago, I. (2008) Electoral coordination strikes again: the 2008 general election in Spain. *Southern European Society and Politics*, 13(3), pp. 363–375.

Vavreck, L. (2009) *The Message Matters: The Economy and Presidential Campaigns* (Princeton: Princeton University Press).

Whitten, G. & Palmer, H.D. (1999) Cross-national analyses of economic voting. *Electoral Studies*, 18, pp. 49–67.

Zechmeister, E. (2006) What's left and who's right? A Q-method study of individual and contextual influences on the meaning of ideological labels. *Political Behavior*, 28, pp. 151–173.

Dealignment, De-legitimation and the Implosion of the Two-Party System in Greece: The Earthquake Election of 6 May 2012

EFTICHIA TEPEROGLOU* & EMMANOUIL TSATSANIS**

*University of Mannheim, Germany & University Institute of Lisbon, Portugal; **University Institute of Lisbon, Portugal

ABSTRACT *This article examines the political effects of the global economic recession on Greece in the period from 2010 up to the last weeks of the campaign period for the national elections of 6 May 2012. Our objectives are threefold. First we seek to contextualize its impact and show how the Greek party system departed from the nearly three decades of stability after 2009 and entered a period electoral fluidity and dealignment. Second we identify the demographic and structural characteristics of that dealignment process. Finally we interpret and compare the effect of the economic crisis and other issues on vote choice in the 2012 general election.*

Introduction

The global economic crisis that originated in 2008 in the US financial sector spread quickly across the Atlantic bringing a number of European economies to the brink of collapse. The crisis also shifted into the political domain as governments at the periphery of the Eurozone increasingly faced the prospect of insolvency or "default". Greece was perhaps one of the countries most severely affected by the economic and political fallout from the crisis. The repeated joint EU/IMF "rescue" loans it received marked a desperate attempt by international bodies to stave off a possible default and were accompanied by unprecedented austerity measures and an unpopular debt restructuring deal. Given these dramatic events it was highly likely that voters would seek to vent their frustrations in subsequent elections. Few observers, however, could have predicted the seismic shift that took place in the Greek party system following the crisis.

The dramatic fall in the popularity of PASOK and New Democracy in the May 2009 national election left these two (former) major parties unable to lay claim to

This article makes reference to supplementary material available on the publisher's website at http://dx.doi.org/10.1080/17457289.2014.892495

a majority of seats in parliament and thus to form a coalition government. This result occurred even with the 50-seat bonus for the top-ranked party that was designed to secure a single-party majority in parliament. The refusal of the Coalition of Radical Left (SYRIZA) and of the Democratic Left to participate in a coalition government meant that Greeks had to return to the polls in June. This time the 50-seat bonus awarded to the first party saw the system move towards a new configuration of two-partyism, with New Democracy and SYRIZA sharing power.

At first glance the two elections appear to constitute textbook cases of economic voting. The economic crisis Greece faced was the most serious it had encountered since the end of the civil war in 1949. The dismal state of the economy provided a backdrop not only for the election but seeped into all aspects of social life and public discourse. The PASOK government that presided over the explosion of the debt bomb and negotiated the terms of the first bailout deal in 2010, saw its vote share decline dramatically from 44% in October 2009 to just over 13% in May 2012 and a further percentage point in June. Much of the decline of PASOK was picked up, not by New Democracy, but by smaller parties of the left, SYRIZA in particular, which saw its share increase dramatically to 16% in May 2012 and 27% the following month.

On the surface the causal narrative thus appears fairly straightforward. The electorate attributed the blame for the crisis to the main incumbent party and punished it accordingly for its poor economic record. Beyond this immediate outcome, however, given the extreme nature of the economic crisis experienced in Greece there is a question of whether it had deeper system-level effects that resulted in more than just short-term electoral losses for the incumbent. Our argument is that the economic crisis in Greece has acted as a catalyst for the acceleration of longer-term processes in much the same way as the *Tangentopoli* affair[1] triggered the transformation of the Italian party system after 1992. The growing levels of political cynicism and antiparty sentiments, especially among the post-authoritarian generation in Greece, we contend were reinforced by the crisis and turned indifference into open hostility towards the political class, and specifically towards the two major parties (PASOK and New Democracy). This outrage was particularly strong among the younger generation which, largely unconstrained by the affective ties of their parents and grandparents to specific parties, gravitated to newer anti-system variants that were sceptical or even overtly hostile towards parliamentary politics in general.

The widening nature of the debate further underscored its deeper systemic implications. After a few months the debate shifted from the government's plan to deal with the crisis and issues of economic performance to concerns over a loss of national sovereignty and the merits of EU membership. Within the opposition and the heterogeneous protest movement, attention centred on what was seen as the endemic corruption of the political class and alternatives to parliamentary rule. Furthermore, there was a growing preoccupation with immigration control and the protection of national identity and the Greek way of life.

The goal of this article is to examine the argument that the effects of the recent global economic crisis on Greek politics went much deeper than conventional economic voting models would presume, i.e. a shift in voter preferences in a given election to punish those parties responsible. Instead the crisis provoked a serious fracture and significant reconfiguration of the existing party system. We test this argument by presenting a series of over-time and cross-sectional analyses of voting patterns in the Third Republic. First we contrast the nearly three decades of party system stability with the post-2009 period to show how a new era of dealignment and fluidity emerged after the economic crisis hit. Specifically we use aggregate and individual-level indicators to highlight the discontinuities in the pre- and post-crisis party system and contextualize these changes within the wider society and Greek political culture. In a second step we probe more deeply into the post-2009 situation and identify the demographic and structural characteristics associated with the dealignment process. Finally we trace the relative impact of a range of issues that dominated the spring 2012 electoral campaign. Here we show how the shift in political discourse from economic performance issues to highly contentious and polarizing socio-cultural issues affected the electoral choice of voters.

The Greek Third Republic and the Stability of Two-Party Rule

The Third Republic established in Greece in 1974 brought to an end a seven-year period of dictatorship and against expectations saw the emergence of one of the most stable two-party systems in Europe. Indeed the dominance of the parties led some commentators to label the Third Republic a "*partitocrazia*" (Anthopoulos, 2008: 113), in the vein of the Italian First Republic. At its core stood the two major parties – the socialist PASOK and right-wing New Democracy – which structured political competition firmly along the left–right axis. Indeed this cleavage has been a defining characteristic of Greek politics for most of the twentieth century and has contributed to a sense of continuity in Greek politics despite the changes in political regime and political parties.[2] As Gunther (2005: 270) states, only the left–right stance of the parties has served as a significant inhibitor of inter-bloc volatility in Greece.

The steady alternation of the two major parties in government since 1974 was further supported by the extreme majoritarianism engineered into the Greek electoral system and was broken only by two short-lived coalitions in 1989. This stable duopoly allowed for the return of several features of early parliamentary life in Greece in the nineteenth century. Specifically PASOK and New Democracy operated a modernized version of the patron–client system with party linkages replacing personalized ties. Both parties were dominated by charismatic leaders who relied on populist rhetoric and were run in a top-down fashion. The existing strength of political identities shaped by past regime crises and buttressed by existing clientelist ties meant that levels of party attachment were high from the early days of the new regime (Featherstone, 2005: 229; Haralambis, 1989) and led to the formation of highly durable parallel networks of "left" and "right" political blocs. In every national election from the 1970s until the start of the twenty-first century New Democracy and PASOK gathered well over 80% of the vote. This all came to a dramatic end, however, in the aftermath of the global financial crisis and Greek economic meltdown. The parliamentary elections of 2007 and 2009 saw the combined vote for

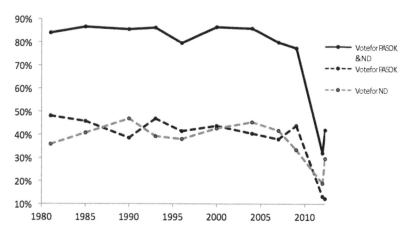

Figure 1. The collapse of the stable two-party system: PASOK and New Democracy
percentages in national elections, 1981–2012
Note: May and June elections 2012.

the two major parties for the first time fall slightly below 80% (79.9% and 77.4% respectively). In 2012, however, it collapsed completely to less than one-third.

Figure 1 shows this history of stability and precipitous decline after 2010.

A consequence of the very predictable swing in power between the two main parties led to the creation of a vastly inflated state bureaucracy in which party loyalties superseded administrative considerations. Every change of party in government saw a large number of new appointments for the loyalists of the winning party at both higher and lower levels of the public sector. Constitutional constraints meant that the existing civil servants could not be removed. The result was that election after election, the size of public sector continued to swell as it sought to accommodate the supporters of both parties. As well as rewarding supporters after an election the patronage system was also used by the incumbent party to recruit new employees into the public sector in advance of the next polling day. This cycle of appointments and the use of the state budget in order to attract votes and facilitate a return to power gave rise to what Sotiropoulos saw as the conventional "pump priming" economic-electoral cycle with "a clientelist twist" (Sotiropoulos, 2012: 42). Under such an arrangement parties sought to curry favour and win votes through direct changes in individuals' personal and household economic welfare and their professional advancement.

Given this inter-linkage of personal and party fortunes in Greece it is clear that the explosion of the fiscal time bomb did more than undermine confidence in the major parties to manage the economy, it severely hampered their ability to perform their traditional patronage functions. Until 2009 it was expected that the party in power would offer job openings to its supporters, even fixed-term or project-based ones. However in late 2009 the newly elected PASOK government – under pressure to cut public spending – drastically cut the number of patronage appointments (Sotiropoulos,

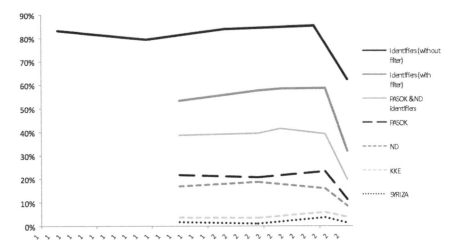

Figure 2. Party identification in Greece, 1985–2011
Note: The questionnaires by EKKE, OPINION and MRB ask respondents their degree of proximity to each party separately, thus tending to show always higher levels of party identifiers and allowing for multiple party identifications. The questionnaires by CNEP and ESS use filter questions, thus allowing for unique party identifications only.
Sources: EKKE 1985, OPINION 1993; CNEP 1996; MRB 2000, 2011; ESS 1, 2, 4, 5.

2012: 44). This failure broke faith with the "clientelist social contract" that had legitimized and reproduced two-party rule in modern democratic Greece since its foundation and led to a fracturing of the duopoly.

Figure 2 shows this critical juncture and sudden decline in party identification very clearly. The data also reveal that the downward trend is not limited to the two major parties.

The Undercurrents of Political Culture: De-legitimation as Harbinger of Dealignment

The demise of the two-party system in 2012, as one might expect, did not occur in a vacuum. Despite suffering some ups and downs since its foundation, public trust and confidence in political institutions in the Third Republic have been relatively high compared with other nations in Southern Europe (Kafetzis, 1994; Pantelidou-Malouta, 1990). Indeed by 2004, trust in institutions and satisfaction with democracy had reached a peak. This was the year the Olympic Games were held in Greece. The country was moving along the path of integration within the European Union and had experienced several consecutive years of sustained growth. The positive outlook was short-lived, however. A series of corruption scandals beset the New Democracy government from 2007 to 2009 and the explosion of the sovereign debt crisis in 2010 saw a complete collapse of citizen confidence in the main executive and institutions of government and parliament.

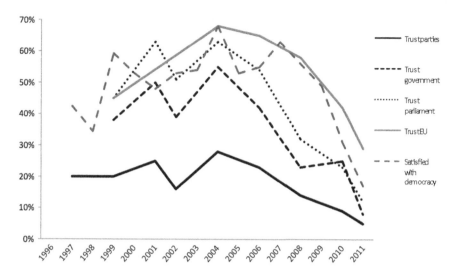

Figure 3. Satisfaction with democracy and trust towards political institutions and European Union, 1997–2011.
Source: Eurobarometer series

Figure 3 shows this rising disaffection very clearly by mapping trend data in Greek political attitudes. Here we see how trust in parliament, which had always been quite high, plummeted to almost single-digit percentages by 2011. Figure 3 also shows the sharp drop in support for the EU within Greece that has took hold following the debt crisis. Greece has traditionally been one of the most pro-EU countries which is not surprising given the considerable economic benefits accrued from membership. It was equally unsurprising, therefore, that the pro-EU sentiments have eroded in the face of growing perceptions of a German-controlled EU that is imposing harsh fiscal measures on Greece and increasing their financial pain.

A final important trend reported in Figure 3 is that alongside a decline of faith in governing institutions there appears to be increasing disillusionment with the demo-cratic regime writ large. Satisfaction with democracy in Greece according to these figures has fallen to historically low levels. While one cannot assume a straightfor-ward trade-off between the level of support for democracy and a preference for authoritarian solutions the question of whether Greece has entered a new era of declining regime legitimacy appears now to have become a serious question for debate. A recent study (conducted by Panteion University) of supporters of the recent anti-government protests for instance revealed that less than a quarter of the sample supported the idea that the best way to take decisions is through elected gov-ernments and representative democratic institutions (24%); the remainder preferred referendums and people's assemblies or technocrats and strong leaders (58% and 17% respectively) (Kollia, 2012).

Further evidence of this de-legitimation of the Greek regime has emerged with the sudden growth in popular support for the extreme-right Golden Dawn party. Having gained a comfortable entry into parliament with around 7% of the popular vote it has continued to attract around 10% of support in public opinion polls in 2013, emerging as the third largest party behind New Democracy and SYRIZA. Despite a belated attempt to dissociate themselves from Nazism, its success underscores the view that deeper anti-system views are taking hold within the Greek electorate. The party's rhetoric attacks what it perceives as a corrupt *pseudo-democracy* and it organizes its members into militia-style groups who wear trademark black t-shirts and routinely exercise street-level violence against immigrants, homosexuals and their political opponents. Rather than deterring supporters this combination of anti-democratic rhetoric and violent grassroots mobilization against both elites and mar-ginalized "out-groups" appears to have won over a sizeable minority of the Greek electorate.[3] The murder of Pavlos Fyssas, a leftist hip-hop artist, in September 2013 led to the arrest of a member of Golden Dawn and the subsequent arrest of its leadership on charges of conspiracy to create a criminal organization. As of January 2014, the leader of Golden Dawn, Nikos Michaloliakos, remains in prison awaiting his trial. The criminal allegations, however, do not appear to have affected the party's polling strength which has remained stable despite a short-lived drop in October immediately after the murder of Fyssas.

Partisanship Before and After the Onset of the Crisis

As noted earlier, one of the defining features of the Greek Third Republic has been the relatively high levels of party identification it has experienced compared with other Western democracies. The fragmentation of the party system in the post-crisis era we argue constitutes a profound shift in Greek politics and is one that takes us beyond conventional economic voting explanations of electoral outcomes. In taking this wider approach, however, we do not discount or overlook the fact that other more immediate responses to punish incumbents may also have occurred.

The Changing Backdrop of Partisanship

In this section we examine the changing patterns of party identification mapped above in Figure 2 more closely and potential explanations for them using a range of data sources from 1985 to 2012 (for a detailed list and abbreviations of data sources see Appendix 1). Using these sources we can see that one of the more obvious suspects in promoting this dealignment and fluidity – age – is indeed an important factor in the process. Table 1 shows that party identification has fallen most notably among younger cohorts that were socialized in the post-authoritarian era of the Third Repub-lic. Party identification is typically a psychological attachment that intensifies throughout the life-cycle with repeated voting (see Campbell et al., 1960; Converse, 1969: 143). Thus we would naturally expect to find lower levels of this attitude among younger voters. However, the over-time evidence we assemble from three

Table 1. Age and party identification ("close to at least one party")

	18–24	25–34	35–44	45–54	55–64	65+
1985	81%	80%	84%	83%	88%	84%
1993	75%	75%	87%	89%	89%	89%
2011	51%	59%	63%	64%	71%	74%

Sources: EKKE1985, OPINION 1993, MRB 2011.

time points (1985, 1993 and 2011) suggests that non-identification found among younger people in the more recent election is more than simply a life-cycle effect.

Alongside the decrease in partisanship within the Greek electorate other related symptoms of political malaise can be seen to be gathering pace over the same time period. Accompanying the decline of partisanship is an increase in the proportion of voters that are unwilling place themselves on the ideological left–right axis. Since the return of democracy in the 1970s studies have shown that Greeks were more likely to place themselves on the left–right axis than voters in other new democracies in Southern Europe, i.e. Portugal and Spain (see Freire, 2006: 158). The 1985 EKKE study reports that an overwhelming majority (91%) of the sample selected a position on the left–right axis. This declined to around 80% by 2000 (MRB, 2000) where it continued to hover for the rest of the decade (ESS 1, 2, 4). By 2011 it had dropped again, with only 74% (MRB, 2011) declaring a left–right position. While this trend can be seen to some extent as a natural outcome following the consolidation of democracy and normalization in levels of party polarization, the sharp drop after 2010 is nonetheless striking. Furthermore the relationship of age to the disjuncture is clearly notable. In 1985 the youngest two age cohorts (18–24 and 25–34) both displayed similar or higher rates of self-placement compared to other age groups (i.e. above 90%). By 2011 the figures for these cohorts have fallen markedly with only 53% of 18–24 year olds and 68% of the 25–34 age group seeing themselves as holding a left-right position (MRB, 2011).

Correlates of Major Party Identification

Through multivariate analyses it is possible to develop a more complex understanding of the drivers of the patterns we have observed above in party identification and the relative importance of age. For the period 2003–2011, we use data from rounds 1, 2, 4 and 5 of the European Social Survey. In our multivariate models we include socio-demographic variables, such as sex (female), age, education, employment status (self-employed, unemployed and retired), place of residence (rural areas), union membership and church attendance. From existing research we know that there are several socio-structural variables that are important in predicting identification with the two major parties. In particular attachments towards both PASOK and New Democracy tend to be formed by members of older cohorts who reside in rural areas and tend to be more religious (Gunther & Montero, 2001; Vernardakis, 2011: 160–165). In addition, we include measures of political attitudes such as interest and left–right self-placement (measured as proximity to the centre) along with other relevant attitudinal variables repeated across the series such as the evaluation of one's present household economic situation,[4] the cultural impact of immigration, trust in parliament[5] and preferences concerning legal response to anti-democratic political parties.

We conduct the multinomial logit analyses by survey year with major party identification (PASOK and New Democracy) as the reference category. The full results of the regression analysis are reported in Tables 1–4 of the Online Appendix (see <www.doi.org/10.1080/17457289.2014.892495>). To more efficiently explore these findings further we looked at the marginal effects of the key variables of interest

Table 2. Voting intention, 2012. Multinomial logit with governing coalition parties (PASOK and ND) as reference category (N=130)

Predictors	Left opposition parties			Right opposition partiesll		
	B (std. error)	z	odds ratio	B (std. error)	z	odds ratio
Female	−1.04 (0.327)***	−3.18	0.354	−0.687 (0.380) †	−1.81	0.503
Age	−0.572 (0.204)**	−2.81	0.564	−1.14 (0.227)***	−5.02	0.321
Education	−0.483 (0.141)***	−3.43	0.617	−0.226 (0.174)	−1.30	0.797
EU positive	−0.656 (0.208)**	−3.16	0.519	−0.313 (0.234)	−1.34	0.731
Civil disobedience	0.768 (0.173)***	4.43	2.156	0.323 (0.201)	1.61	1.381
Immigration control	−0.888 (0.243)***	−3.66	0.411	0.494 (0.280) †	1.77	1.639
Economic liberalism	−0.722 (0.250)**	−2.89	0.486	0.136 (0.289)	0.47	1.146
Church–state separation	0.470 (0.132)***	3.57	1.600	0.113 (0.146)	0.78	1.120
Bailout positive	−0.476 (0.201)**	−2.37	0.621	−0.508 (0.228)**	−2.23	0.602
Intercept	9.52 (2.20)***	4.65		3.42 (2.47)		
N	170			62		
	Cox & Snell Pseudo-R²=0.50					

Note: †p<0.1, *p<0.5; **p<0.01; ***p<0.001
Left opposition parties: KKE, SYRIZA, Democratic Left.
Right opposition parties: Independent Greeks, Golden Dawn.
Source: HelpMeVote.

in each survey on the probability of three outcomes: expressing proximity to either PASOK or New Democracy; expressing proximity to one of the smaller parties, or expressing no proximity to parties whatsoever. Figure 4 reports the change in probabilities in each of the three outcomes caused by an increase of one standard deviation for each attitudinal variable (in each of the four ESS surveys), while holding the other variables at their mean.

The results show that evaluations of the household economic situation have only a weak effect on partisanship for both major and minor parties. Anti-system attitudes are by contrast among the most important attitudinal variables in predicting partisanship among minor party adherents and this holds true across the last decade. Trust in parliament, willingness to accept anti-democratic parties (and of course, the interest in politics) all emerge as the most important discriminating variables between major party identifiers and small party identifiers. Viewed more generally, however, the attitudinal variables do not appear to have a particularly strong impact on partisanship. We turn next to look at the impact of economic concerns on vote choice in 2012.

Towards an Explanation of Voting Behaviour in the May 2012 Election

The economy clearly weighed heavily on voters' minds in the lead up to the May elections. In March 2012, 91% of the public gave negative retrospective evaluations of their household economic situation according to opinion surveys (Public Issue 101). A few weeks before the election almost all (94%) Greeks believed that "things are getting worse in the country" (MRB, 2012), which was an increase of over 20% compared to the 72% that felt the same way earlier in March 2010 (MRB, 2010). During the same period, the two most important problems were the economy (47%) and unemployment (24%) (Metron, 2012).

Pessimism over the economy had clearly been building for some time. Indeed the election of 2009 in many ways appears to have exhibited some of the classic traits of economic voting in terms of attribution of blame and the direction of swing voting. According to survey data from late 2009 the economy and unemployment were the two most important issues in the minds of voters and 80% of voters considered the performance of New Democracy as the incumbent between 2007 and 2009 as bad or very bad (CSES III). New Democracy received one-third of the vote, its worst electoral performance in its history other than its subsequent loss in 2012 and the major opposition party, PASOK, reaped the benefits by capturing 44% of the vote, up almost 6% from the 2007 election.

Despite the evidence of its increasing scope and applicability, the study of economic voting in Greece is limited. The work that has been done prior to the crisis shows the relationship between economic conditions and attitudes to governing parties is a complex one. Freire and Costa Lobo (2005) used Eurobarometer data to examine economic voting in Southern Europe between 1985 and 1999. Their analysis concluded that sociotropic and egocentric economic perceptions were significant determinants of voting behaviour in Greece and were more important than social class. However, economic perceptions did not follow the expected direction

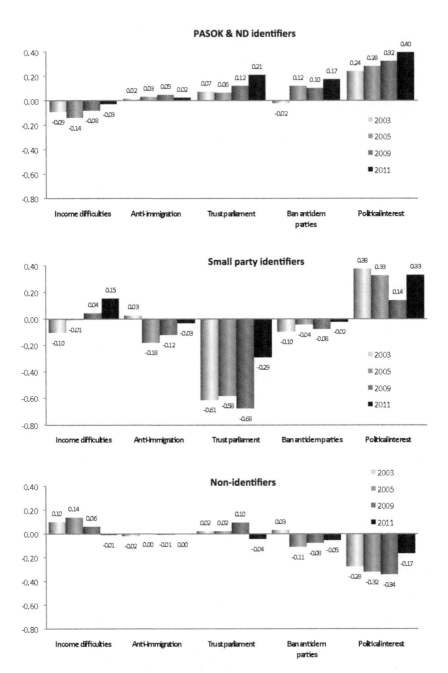

Figure 4. Predicted proportional change to probability of expressing closeness to parties caused by a one-standard deviation increase in predictor.
Source: ESS 1,2,4,5
Note: Effects when other variables are being held constant at mean values.

based on objective economic indicators (GDP growth, inflation and unemployment), except for the correlation between the perceptions of personal finances and GDP annual variation (Freire & Costa Lobo, 2005: 513–514). One of the few exclusive studies of Greece on the question of economic voting shows that economic expectations were mediated by partisanship in the national election of 2004 and the European Parliament election of 2009 (Nezi, 2012: 504).

Post-crisis work by Kosmidis (2013) using long-term aggregate data has added a further layer of explanation to the economic voting model in Greece by introducing the impact of international or external actors. After the first "memorandum" was voted on by parliament in May 2010 he argues that a shift took place in the way that voters assigned responsibility for the state of the economy, from supranational institutions to the national government. The idea that economic voting increases as blame attribution shifts from external agents towards the national government is consistent with the literature. However, within this picture he detects a more complex curvilinear relationship in the Greek case. Specifically, through his time series analysis he reveals that attribution of blame to the national government was actually lower prior to the bailout by international lenders but then increased once the package was in place. This rather counter-intuitive finding he explains through reference to a "room to manoeuvre" argument whereby Greek economic conditions deteriorated rapidly causing voters to pay more attention to the issue and who was responsible. As international institutions started to intervene the government suffered some constraints but maintained a limited room to manoeuvre which voters were aware of.

This was then overtaken by events as international lenders were assigned a larger proportion of the blame. Another and complementary interpretation of this relationship could be that the bailout ceased to represent an exclusively economic policy question but became entangled with the much more politically charged question of national sovereignty. In other words, the increased tendency for assignment of responsibility to the national government for economic policy outcomes at a time when it was more constrained than ever can be explained by the fact that the electorate started assigning blame to the national government for ceding sovereignty in key policy areas and international lenders.

Finally a study using individual-level data by Karyotis and Rüdig (2013) in late 2010 has challenged these conclusions and added an additional variable into the mix. Contrary to Kosmidis the authors find that blame attribution exerted no significant impact on vote intention – at least during the early months after the voting of the first bailout deal – while egocentric and prospective sociotropic economic variables, did have some impact. The most crucial variable in determining future voting choice, however, in fact turned out to be acceptance of the government's "security discourse". The authors define this as a rhetoric which identifies an "urgent, existential threat" facing the nation and is generally employed by governments when trying to deflect blame attribution for the imposition of harsh austerity measures, by presenting them as inevitable and necessary for the survival of the national community (Karyotis & Rüdig, 2013: 4–5). In other words, the crucial variable to explain vote choice in the Greek case was not conventional variables related to perceived government

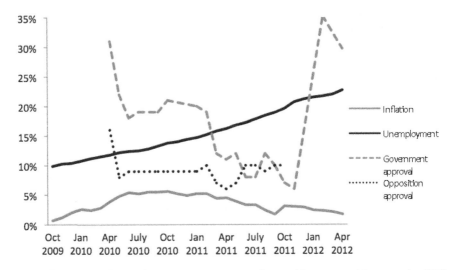

Figure 5. Inflation, unemployment, government and opposition approval between the 2009 and 2012 elections.
Sources: Inflation data from Hellenic Statistic Authority; unemployment data from OECD; Government and opposition approval data from Public Issue time-series

performance and attribution of blame, but the extent to which an individual accepted the government's line that the bailout deal was the least worst of available options.

The Impact of the Bailout Deal and Position Issues on Voting Choice

Trend data leading up to the May 2012 election reported in Figure 5 show that the relationship between economic and political evaluations was not a straightforward one. Here we juxtapose standard macroeconomic performance figures against government and opposition approval ratings from the end of 2009 until April 2012.

The two economic indicators alongside the contraction in GDP (not reported) capture the downward spiral of the Greek economy since the onset of the debt crisis, particularly the rates of unemployment. In 2009 the unemployment rate was in single-digits and within the space of three years it had exceeded 25%. During the same period, as expected the approval ratings for the PASOK government experienced an equally steep decline, falling to single-digits. However, interestingly the opposition party fared no better. There was a short spike in government approval following the formation of the coalition government between PASOK and New Democracy and replacement of George Papandreou as head of government by the "technocrat" Lucas Papademos in 2011. The optimism about the new coalition government under Papademos was very short-lived and soon after government approval ratings entered a steep downward trajectory where they remained until the election in May.

In order to further explore the impact of economic factors on the election outcome we move on to conduct a multivariate analysis which examines their impact relative to the attitudinal and external variables highlighted as important in the extant literature (see Appendix 2 for the survey items' precise question wording and variable construction). Our analysis is based on original data collected in late April 2012 in which we have a measure of vote choice (as measured by vote intention) in the May 2012 national election. Due in part to low frequencies of individual party choice in our sample we created three aggregated categories of party voting intention as our dependent variable which reflected the key divisions that emerged during the campaign. The first category corresponds to the two former major parties (the incumbent, pro-bailout parties so to speak), the second one to the leftist opposition parties (KKE, SYRIZA and Democratic Left), and the third to rightist opposition parties (Independent Greeks and Golden Dawn).

In terms of the independent variables, none of the datasets available to us contained any of the items that are typically found in National Election Studies that tap into "valence issues", i.e. items that capture evaluations of the state of the economy and government performance. However, the dataset we used for this section of the analysis did include a rich array of items on issues relating to the EU and immigration and also several items that measured views on the bailout loan and the attached "memorandum" (i.e. its inevitability, its necessity, its desirability and its long-term prospects). Such questions are arguably just as useful, and possibly even more effective at capturing "valence" views on the economy in this context. During such an extreme economic downturn these sociotropic or "meta" level evaluations tend to be uniformly negative and thus their power to discriminate over different outcomes is significantly reduced. Views on the two memoranda that were voted prior to the 2012 elections are more contextualized and condense a range of attitudes relating to government performance and the prospective state of the economy at this particular juncture in Greece's history.

Given the structure of our dependent variable, multinomial logit was used to predict outcomes. The model also includes the conventional socio-demographic predictors as controls (sex, age, education). The full model results are presented in Table 2.

As expected the bailout variable is significant in both models, showing that it was a clear factor in pushing voters away from the two main parties and towards opposition parties on both the right and left. That said, however, another clear finding from the analysis is that there was much more dividing the voters of the major parties and their left-wing opposition than there was dividing the former and supporters for the right-wing opposition parties. Other than age and views on the bailout voters for PASOK and ND shared a similar outlook to those supporting their small right-wing counterparts. Between the larger parties and the smaller leftist parties, however, there were clear differences on view of the EU, the handling of protest, immigration controls and economic openness.

Figure 6 presents the marginal effects for the key attitudinal predictors on choice of party bloc.

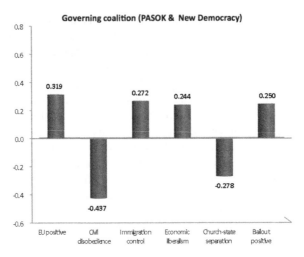

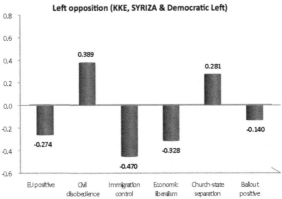

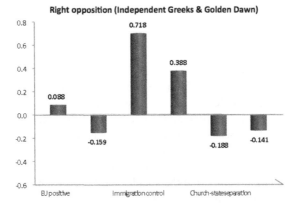

Figure 6. Predicted proportional change to probability of voting for party bloc caused by one-standard deviation increase in the predictor.

Note: Effects when other variables are being held constant at mean values

Source: HelpMeVote

The results are compelling in that they confirm that voters were discriminating among parties based on a range of issues and not simply on economic performance grounds. The variable measuring support for the bailout deal shows that it mattered for voters for all parties and followed the expected direction in that more positive attitudes are associated with support for PASOK and New Democracy while those who are critical are more likely to support the opposition (both left and right). Beyond support for the bailout, however, positive attitudes towards external bodies such as the EU and for maintaining internal order actually appear to have an even stronger effect in generating support for the coalition parties.

Positive stances towards immigration control are by far the strongest predictors of support for right-wing opposition party voters, while the reverse holds for voters of left-wing opposition parties. More generally left-wing voters have the most sharply defined profile in comparison to the other two groups of voters. Supporters of left-wing opposition parties were distinguished by their strong opposition to economic liberalism, the EU and the euro as well as support for civil disobedience and separation of church and state. Aside from immigration, however, only economically liberal positions stand out as increasing the probability of voting for a right-wing opposition party. The results confirm the conclusion drawn from Table 2 of the congruence in the voters for the two major parties and for right-wing opposition parties. The only difference between them is over intensity to which the issue of immigration mattered and, of course, the directionality of attitudes towards the bailout deals. Thus it seems that while there are deep ideological divisions separating voters of leftist parties from those supporting the two centrist parties, it is a combination of anti-bailout attitudes and the need for tougher immigration measures that moved voters away from the two major parties and towards the smaller opposition parties of the right.

As a final check on the impact of the memoranda versus other issue positions on the support for the various party blocs we re-ran the multinomial logit with an additional two more memorandum-related questions to create a multi-item measure that captured evaluations of the bailout deals in Greece.[6] The incremental changes to the pseudo-R^2 reported in Figure 7 decisively show that the memorandum and bailout were less influential in determining the vote for the two former major parties than

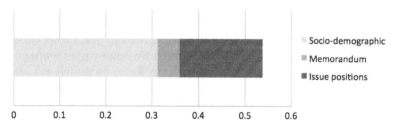

Figure 7. Incremental Cox & Snell Pseudo-R^2 (reference category: PASOK or ND voting intention).
Source: HelpMeVote

other non-economic issues. While one might be tempted from these findings to conclude that the economic crisis took a back seat in the 2012 election, this appears to be too simplistic. Instead the results indicate that the main result of the crisis was to re-politicize a number of divisive issues that had themselves been simmering in the background such as questions of relations to the European Union, social peace, as well as national identity and immigration.

Discussion and Conclusions

The results of the May 2012 election marked a watershed in the political history of the Greek Third Republic. Support for the two main parties that had dominated politics in the post-authoritarian era crumbled to the point that for the first time in their existence their combined vote share did not exceed a third of those cast. The subsequent June election and the 50-seat bonus awarded to the first party helped to further dislodge the old two-party system and usher in a new configuration. This shift in the political landscape as we have shown here was in part a result of sovereign debt crisis which affected Greece more than any other country in Europe. However, it was also clearly intertwined with the deepening of other longer term cultural divisions in Greek society and increased cynicism towards elites and established democratic institutions.

The continuing fluidity of the political landscape makes it difficult to offer any predictions about the process of realignment. The move towards a new two-party system could easily be reversed, particularly if the long awaited reform of the electoral system is finally pursued. Specifically, if the new electoral law removes the current 50-seat bonus awarded to the first party and increases the proportionality in the distribution of parliamentary seats, the strategic incentive that pushed so many voters to switch their vote in the election of June (compared to May) in favour of New Democracy or SYRIZA will cease to exist. That said two important and potentially significant outcomes do appear to be detectable at present. The first is the collapse of the mainstream left in the shape of PASOK which appears to have been hit hardest by recent events. This was no doubt in part because the debt-bomb exploded in its hands. However, the party also failed to undertake the type of public purging of its leadership ranks that its long time right-wing rival New Democracy insisted upon after its defeat in 2009.

The second and perhaps less obvious outcome is the more contentious political climate that has developed since the economic depression. Since 2009 Greece has entered a phase of triangular polarization marked by centrist pro-European forces (represented by the old major parties), anti-austerity forces on the left and xenophobic, anti-bailout forces on the right. The consequence is that political debate appears to have moved away from questions of the performance and competence of parties and their leaders and is increasingly centred on more fundamental and politically polarizing questions. Whether this increasingly fragmented political environment can find a new consensus now remains a key question for future research to investigate.

Acknowledgements

We would like to thank the editor of this special issue, Pedro Magalhães, for his consistently valuable remarks on the various drafts of this article (which started as a conference paper that was presented at Georgetown in April 2012), as well as Rachel Gibson and the two reviewers for their insightful comments and helpful suggestions. We are grateful to Elias Nicolakopoulos and Theodore Chadjipadelis for the permission of using the MRB 2011 and HelpMeVote data respectively.

Notes

1. *Tangentopoli* (Italian for bribeville) was the name generally used to refer to the corruption based political system that ruled Italy until the *mani pulite* (clear hands) investigation delivered it a deadly blow in 1992, leading to the demise of the DC and of the Socialist Party (PSI).
2. Only one party from the pre-authoritarian period remained after 1974 – the KKE (Communist Party).
3. In fact, after a televised episode of violence carried out by Golden Dawn's MP Elias Kasidiaris against two female MPs of SYRIZA and KKE during a morning talk show, there was a reversal of the party's seeming waning electoral appeal at the time (Ellinas, 2013: 17).
4. The question from the ESS main questionnaire that we are using in our analysis is "Which of the descriptions on comes closest to how you feel about your household's income nowadays?" The 11-point sociotropic economic evaluation scale was excluded from our analysis due to the high negative skewness of the distribution in 2011 and lack of sufficient variation in the sample.
5. The only repeated item on the ESS questionnaire which captures orientation towards the European Union is the question concerning trust in the European Parliament. We chose to exclude this variable due to high observed levels of collinearity with the "trust in parliament" variable.
6. The two more memorandum-related questions are: "Much of what is included in the Memoranda ought to have been done long ago" and "it is possible to renegotiate the Memorandum". The answers were given on a five-point scale, 1 = Fully disagree to 5 = Fully agree (source: HelpMeVote).

References

Anthopoulos, C. (2008) The Greek party system as particracy, in: X. Kontiadis & C. Anthopoulos (eds) *The Crisis of the Greek Political System* (Athens: Papazisis), pp. 111–138 (in Greek).

Campbell, A., Converse, P., Miller, W. & Stokes, D. (1960) *The American Voter* (New York: Wiley).

Converse, P. (1969) Of time and partisan stability. *Comparative Political Studies*, 2, pp. 139–172.

Ellinas, A. (2013) The rise of Golden Dawn: the new face of the far right in Greece. *South European Society and Politics*, 18(4), pp. 543–565.

Featherstone, K. (2005) Introduction: "modernization" and the structural constraints of Greek politics. *West European Politics*, 28(2), pp. 223–241.

Freire, A. (2006) Left-right ideological identities in new democracies: Greece, Portugal and Spain in the Western European context. *Pôle Sud*, 25, pp. 153–173.

Freire, A. & Costa Lobo, M. (2005) Economics, ideology and vote: Southern Europe, 1985–2000. *European Journal of Political Research*, 44, pp. 493–518.

Gunther, R. (2005) Parties and electoral behaviour in Southern Europe. *Comparative Politics*, 37(3), pp. 253–275.

Gunther, R. & Montero, J.R. (2001) The anchors of partisanship: a comparative analysis of voting behavior in four Southern European democracies, in: P.N. Diamandouros & R. Gunther (eds) *Parties, Politics, and Democracy in the New Southern Europe* (Baltimore: Johns Hopkins University Press), pp. 83–152.

Haralambis, D. (1989) *Clientelistic Relations and Populism* (Athens: Exantas) (in Greek).

Kafetzis, P. (1994) Political crisis and political culture, in: N. Demertzis (ed.) *Greek Political Culture Today* (Athens: Exantas), pp. 217–251 (in Greek).

Karyotis, G. & Rüdig, W. (2013) Blame and punishment? The electoral politics of extreme austerity in Greece. Political Studies (doi:10.1111/1467-9248.12076) (in press).

Kollia, Eleftheria (2012, 22 July). The square was filled with … indignants. *To Vima*. Retrieved from: http://www.tovima.gr/society/article/?aid=467898 (in Greek)

Kosmidis, S. (2013) Government constraints and economic voting in Greece. *GreeSE Paper No.70.* Hellenic Observatory Papers on Greece and Southeast Europe.

Nezi, R. (2012) Economic voting under the economic crisis: evidence from Greece. *Electoral Studies*, 31, pp. 498–505.

Pantelidou-Malouta, M. (1990) Greek political culture: aspects and approaches. *Social Studies Review*, Special Issue 75A, pp. 18–57 (in Greek).

Sotiropoulos, D. (2012) A democracy under stress: Greece since 2010. *Taiwan Journal of Democracy*, 8(1), pp. 27–49.

Vernardakis, C. (2011) Political Parties, Elections & Party System: The Transformations of Political Representation, 1990–2010 (Athens: Sakkoulas) (in Greek).

Appendix

Appendix 1. Surveys

No	Title of survey	Research institution/firm	Abbreviation	Fieldwork	Sample
1	"Four Nations Study" (Greece, Italy, Spain and Portugal)	Greek National Center of Social Research (EKKE)	EKKE 1985	06.05.1985-28.5.1985	2,000
2	OPINION No OP.09.93.227	Opinion S.A.	OPINION 1993	23.9.1993-8.10.1993	2,009
3	Comparative National Elections Project-Round 1	Greek National Center of Social Research (EKKE)	CNEP 1996	09.1996- 10.1996	1,196 (1st), 966 (2nd)
4	MRB "Taseis" (Trends)	MRB Hellas	MRB 2000	02.2000	2,000
	European Social Survey-Round 1	Greek National Center of Social Research (EKKE)	ESS 1	29.01.03- 15.03.03	2,566
5	European Social Survey-Round 2	Greek National Center of Social Research (EKKE)	ESS 2	10.01.05-20.03.05	2,406
6	European Social Survey-Round 4	Greek National Center of Social Research (EKKE)	ESS 4	15.07.09-20.11.09	2,072
7	Comparative Study of Electoral Systems Module Three	Aristotle University of Thessaloniki-Department of Political Science	CSES III	10.12.2009-18.12.2009	1,022
8	MRB survey for Real News	MRB Hellas	MRB 2010	26.03.2010-29.03.2010	1,011
9	Public Issue Political Barometer 83	Public Issue S.A.	Public Issue 83	01.10.2010-04.10.2010	1,045
10	European Social Survey-Round 5	Greek National Center of Social Research (EKKE)	ESS 5	06.05.11 to 05.07.11	2,715
11	Public Issue Political Barometers 96	Public Issue S.A.	Public Issue 96	I Wave: 03.11.2011 to 04.11.2011, II Wave:: 07.11.2011 to 10.11.2011	484 (1st), 1,206 (2nd)
12	MRB "Taseis" (Trends)	MRB Hellas	MRB 2011	01.12.2011-08.12.2011	2,000
13	Public Issue Political Barometer 101	Public Issue S.A.	Public Issue 101	8-13/3/2012	1,010
14	Metron Forum April 2012	Metron Analysis	Metron 2012	20.03.12 to 06.04.2012	2,010
15	Preelectoral Survey: "HelpMeVote"	Aristotle University of Thessaloniki-Department of Political Science	HelpMeVote	23-29 April 2012	1,200
16	MRB survey for Real News	MRB Hellas	MRB 2012	07.04.2012 to 10.04.2012	1,008

Appendix 2. Variable construction and question wording for position variables used in multinomial logit

Variable construction	Question wording of selected items
EU positive (9-point additive scale: min 1 – max 5)	• "It is better for Greece to be inside the EU than outside" • "The economy of Greece would have better prospects if it were outside the euro"
Civil disobedience (9-point additive scale: min 1 – max 5)	• "Legislation should be passed to limit public demonstrations" • "I am positive towards acts of civil disobedience and resistance such as the 'I won't pay' movement"
Immigration control (13-point additive scale: min 1 – max 5)	• "Eligibility rules for granting asylum and citizenship need to become stricter" • "First generation immigrants cannot be fully integrated in society" • "More attention needs to be given to the rights of citizens born in Greece by Greek parents"
Economic liberalism (13-point additive scale: min 1 – max 5)	• "Lowering tax rates for businesses would facilitate economic growth" • "In order to combat unemployment, there need to be more flexible forms of employment" • "The NHS can become more efficient if it is partially privatized"
Church–state separation	• "There needs to be complete separation of church and state"
Bailout positive (9-point additive scale: min 1 – max 5)	• "The memoranda agreed with the 'troika' were necessary to avoid bankruptcy" • "The memoranda accumulate more debt without any tangible benefits"

Notes: Variable name indicates directionality of recoding. All answers for attitudinal questions were given on a five-point scale, 1 = *Fully disagree* to 5 = *Fully agree*.
Source: HelpMeVote

The Political Consequences of Blame Attribution for the Economic Crisis in the 2013 Italian National Election

PAOLO BELLUCCI

University of Siena, Italy

ABSTRACT   *This article describes the events that brought about the dismissal of the Berlusconi government in November 2011 and the appointment of a cabinet led by former EU commissioner Mario Monti, before moving to an analysis of how popular perceptions of the economic and political situation have evolved since that time. Relying on an ITANES five-wave inter-electoral panel study, the article shows the EU's growing importance as a divisive political issue. Blaming the EU or the former Berlusconi government as a source of the economic crisis exerted a significant impact on party choice in the 2013 election, while retrospective sociotropic economic evaluations were conditional in their impact on the structure of blame attribution for the economic crisis.*

1. Introduction

The financial and sovereign debt crises that swept throughout (Southern) Europe had many victims. Bankers did not always suffer. But there is no doubt that savers, home-owners, enterprises and laid-off workers were badly affected. National governments meanwhile were trapped in a two-level game between the need to maintain electoral support but also to impose dramatic cuts in state expenditures requested by supranational institutions – the IMF, ECB and EU. Indeed, the onset of the economic crisis and its further unfolding have led to the defeats of several incumbent governments and/or the resignation of executives (Bellucci et al., 2012).

Italy was no exception. On 12 November 2011, Italian premier Silvio Berlusconi stepped down; ironically, it was immediately after having won a parliamentary vote on an austerity budget. He had headed the Italian government for almost a decade.[1] After over a year of rule by a subsequent "technical government" led by Mario Monti, a professor of economics and former EU commissioner to the internal market and competition who was backed by a large coalition of all major parties, the 2013 elections resulted in heavy vote losses for both the right-wing People of Freedom (PoF) (down to 21.3% from the 37.2% polled in 2008) and for the left-wing Democratic Party (DP) (which obtained 25.5% of the vote, likewise far from the 2008's result of 33.1%). Conversely the Five Star Movement (5SM), an anti-political group founded by a comedian-turned-blogger Beppe Grillo, which had contested a national election for the first time, became the second largest party in the house (with 25.1% of the votes). The electoral results showed the greatest vote-swing in the history of the Italian Republic, with an index of aggregate volatility of 39.1%; this was even above the 36.7% level reached in the first election of the Second Republic in 1994 (Chiaramonte & Emanuele, 2013). The bonus provided by the electoral law gave the left coalition a wide majority in the lower house, but not in the senate, and pressed by the re-elected President of the Republic and given the 5SM's unwillingness to enter a cabinet with the left, they had to turn to the centre-right coalition in an effort to form a government coalition sustained by a viable majority. On 29 April 2013, the new Italian premier, Enrico Letta (deputy secretary of the Democratic Party), secured a confidence vote in parliament backed by a grand coalition composed of the main left and right parties and Monti's new centrist party – Scelta Civica – which had polled just 10.8%. See Appendix Table 1 for a listing of the results of the elections most relevant to this analysis.

The electoral results ostensibly show that Italians, facing the severest economic crisis in post-war times, voted against all parties that supported the outgoing technical government, and instead rewarded a new opposition – apparently a clear instance of economic voting. However, the transition from Berlusconi's government to Monti's administration made it rather complex for voters to assign responsibility for the management of the economy. The resignation of the Berlusconi-led rightist government in October 2011 did not in fact follow either an electoral defeat or a negative confidence vote in parliament. Allegedly, it was the result of the erosion of the international markets' confidence in the Italian economic and financial systems, which caused the interest rate of Italian bonds to skyrocket. From this perspective, Berlusconi's resignation was due to a vote of no confidence by rating agencies on Italy. At the same time, Italy's relationship with European institutions – and especially whether to comply with the economic road map Bruxelles and Frankfurt dictated – became a highly divisive political issue, and was quickly associated with a more convincing or lukewarm support expressed in parliament by parties in the 2011–2012 grand coalition for the new non-partisan technocratic government led by Mario Monti.

Public opinion was therefore exposed to a new and puzzling political context in which it was not clear which party, if any, was to be held responsible for ruling the country and managing the economy; where it was not clear whether the source of the economic crisis was mainly domestic or rather international; and where, for the first time, the European issue had reached a domestic (fairly negative) prominence in parties' discourse. A non-partisan government in a context of an international economic crisis clearly makes it difficult for voters to rely on traditional accountability evaluations in forming their judgments, thus directly affecting the importance of valence politics as a source of voting.

Table 1. Evaluation of national economic situation

Year	2001*	2004*	2006*	2008**	2011S***	2011F***	2012 S***	2012F***	2013 W***
Incumbent government	Centre-left	Centre-right	Centre-right	Centre-left	Centre-right	Centre-right	Non-partisan	Non-partisan	Non-partisan
GDP % growth	1.9	1.7	2.2	−1.2	1.3 (1st Q)	−0.5 (4th Q)	−1.7 (1st Q)	−2.8 (4th Q)	−2.3 (1st Q)
National economic situation									
Improved	29.3	4.3	9.6	3.5	6.3	2.0	1.5	5.3	2.6
Same	42.3	21.4	25.9	11.5	22.2	13.8	8.6	12.6	11.0
Worsened	33.8	74.3	64.5	85.0	71.5	84.2	89.9	82.1	86.4
Total	100	100	100	100	100	100	100	100	100

Notes: * ITANES 2001–2004–2006 Panel; ** ITANES 2008 Post-election Survey; *** ITANES 2011–13 Inter-Election Panel; Key: F= fall wave; S= spring wave; W = winter post-election wave.

This article seeks to unravel this complex situation and explain the vote choices of Italians in the 2013 election. To do so it is organized as follows: first, it establishes the principal arguments and develops accompanying hypotheses that account for the impact of blame attribution on voters' political choices; it then provides some context to describe the unfolding of events that "forced" the Berlusconi cabinet to resign. Here we connect public opinion with domestic political elites' behaviour and show how popular perceptions of the economic and political situation evolved in 2011–2012 using data from the ITANES five-wave inter-electoral panel study;[2] finally, we analyse the determinants of party support in the 2013 election, focusing on blame attribution for the economic crisis, and discussing the impact of the economic and financial crises on the political attitudes of Italian public opinion and on their vote choice.

2. Valence Politics and Blame Attribution

Aided by a mixed electoral system law, Italy's political transition in the 1990s saw the emergence of new parties, which formed pre-electoral alliances producing real government alternation between opposing camps for the first time in the history of the Italian Republic. The change in the party system also affected the determinants of voting behaviour, with a decline in the importance of social cleavages (class and religion) and a rising influence of valence politics and performance evaluations (Clarke et al., 2009; Stokes, 1992). With time, Italian voters have come to hold the ruling parties increasingly accountable for the country's social and economic situation, to the extent that performance-related issues largely triggered the four government alternations (between centre-right and centre-left governments) between 1996 and 2008. Popular evaluations of government performance signalled voters' orientations, and the incumbent governments, all of which had an approval rating short of 30%, were defeated in the last four legislative elections (Bellucci, 2012).

The international economic crisis that hit Europe and Italy's economy has greatly affected Italian parties' strategies, and may have also affected voters' capacity to hold them responsible for the management of the economy. Let us analyse first the parties' reaction to the crisis. Its direct impact on the fortunes of the 2008–2011 Berlusconi government was strengthened by some pre-existing erosions of the People of Freedom's cohesiveness. A strong united party could have sustained economic downturns, but a party weakened by splinter groups and by a tarnished leadership (see *infra*) was swept away. The choice not to hold new elections in 2011, however, speaks also to the weakness of the opposition. Although formally attributed to the severity of the economic attacks on Italy's state debt by international markets – which would not have spared Italy by allowing time for a new election – President Napolitano's choice not to dismiss parliament was dictated by the simple fact that the opposition, and mainly the largest party (the Democratic Party), was not ready to wage a new election. Both a consensus on a coalition strategy involving other parties and the choice of a candidate leader endorsed by all potential coalition partners were lacking.

Most importantly, postponing elections and supporting an apparently non-partisan technocratic government implementing harsh, long-overdue market and welfare reforms allowed parties to engage – facing their electorate – in responsibility avoidance, placing the blame on the EU and the government for the severe cuts in state expenditures and raised taxation. But crucially, at the same time, parties could claim responsibility for whatever mitigation parliament may succeed (as it happened) in imposing on the harshest financial measures with an eye to their different electoral constituencies.

Over the course of 2012, political competition hinged therefore on the framing structure with which parties conveyed the policy reforms being enacted by the Monti government to their voters, in an attempt to prime them on where to place responsibility for previous, current and future policies. The former government parties (the PoF and Northern League) have clearly attempted to single out the international markets and Europe as the main culprits of the crisis, whereas former opposition parties have mainly called on the ineffectiveness of the Berlusconi government.

Turning to public opinion, the time that elapsed between Berlusconi's fall and the successive election date may have certainly hampered the virtuous circle of responsibility attribution among retrospective (economic) voters, thus affecting democratic accountability. On the other hand, voters need not necessarily be myopic (Lewis-Beck & Paldam, 2000) when evaluating the political and economic performance according to the reward–punishment model, but could also rely on prospective evaluations. Duch and Stevenson (2008) argue that voters assess parties' past performances to project expectations of future performance. Furthermore, research on blame attribution has previously highlighted how accountability by voters requires a prior attribution of responsibility (Rudolph, 2003). However, the process of assigning responsibility is open to group-serving attribution bias (Fiske & Taylor, 1991), which may shape voters' cognitive processes. Since the attribution of responsibility mediates the effect of policy judgments on voting behaviour (Cutler, 2008), voters' retrospective economic assessments may be conditional on perceptions of responsibility attribution. In this framework, two issues appear relevant to understand the 2013 election results: the extent to which Italian parties were held accountable, and the relative importance attributed to potential domestic or international culprits for the economic crisis.

As to the first point, how can voters attribute responsibility for the country's economic performance to a non-partisan government backed by a grand coalition in a time of harsh international financial crisis? Anderson and Hecht's (2012) analysis of the 2009 German federal election – in a situation where a grand coalition faced an economic crisis – shows tenuous retrospective economic voting, while in contrast, Magalhães' (2012) account of the Portuguese 2011 legislative elections – in a context more similar to Italy as to the seriousness of the economic distress, but with a clear distinction between government and opposition roles – documents greater responsiveness by voters' in evaluating government performance. In both polities, however, the perceived international-external initial source of the economic crisis attenuated the voters' direct attribution of responsibility to domestic political actors, in keeping with research indicating how economic voting may be hampered by the internationalization of the economy, which constrains elected representatives (Duch & Stevenson, 2010; Fernandez-Albertos, 2006; Hellwig, 2008).

As to the second issue, it was crucial for parties to choose to signal to voters either national or international culprits of the crisis. In this context, the European Union has inevitably come to the fore and, for the first time in a country as Europhile as Italy, strong disagreement has been voiced, negatively affecting popular perceptions of the European Union (Bellucci & Conti, 2012). Mr Monti's policies have in fact been (rightly) interpreted by both media and parties as the implementation of EU/ECB initiatives whose enforcement or not constitutes a strategic choice – a policy platform – for parties competing for government in the future. The electoral visibility of the EU has therefore been greatly heightened, exposing two conditions which previous research has singled out as catalysts of EU issue voting: salience and partisan conflict over Europe (de Vries, 2007). In turn, the EU's visibility in domestic politics could have further depressed economic voting, to the extent that voters perceive the EU as responsible for national policy, and ruling parties are held less accountable for economic performance (Costa Lobo & Lewis-Beck, 2012).

Finally, partisanship could mediate the evaluation of the economy and blame attribution. In contrast to the established literature on economic voting (see Lewis-Beck & Stegmaier, 2007), recent research has questioned the direct link between economic evaluation and voting choice, suggesting a reverse causation stemming from prior partisan beliefs (Anderson, 2007; Evans & Pickup, 2010). Although far from established, this issue has prompted an analogous concern regarding voters' cognitive process of blame attribution – "selective attribution" (Tilley & Hobolt, 2011). Accordingly, partisanship would not only "colour" an evaluation of the economy, but crucially, would also shape the popular perception of who is responsible for policy outcomes. Moreover, voters appear to use available information selectively depending on the credibility of the source; in the UK, the EU scores lower on credibility than the national government and parties (Hobolt et al., 2013). The combination of partisan heuristics employed by voters and a tarnished image of the EU could then produce perceptual biases in responsibility attribution among Italian voters, with potentially highly significant electoral consequences.

The foregoing suggests that valence politics might be a tenuous direct source of voting choice in 2013. Retrospective economic evaluation should exert a moderate or null direct impact on voting. Assigning responsibility for the crisis should, on the other hand, be directly linked to voting choice, with partisans of right (left) parties supporting them when seeing international (domestic) actors responsible for the crisis. Finally, interactions between retrospective economic assessments and responsibility attribution to international or domestic actors should also emerge as a significant predictor. The expectation is that economic concerns associated with assigning responsibility for the crisis to international actors (EU and financial markets) should favour the right-wing PoF, while the opposite would be the case for the left-wing DP.

Before moving on to the analysis, it is of interest to understand how public opinion has evolved during the transition period after the fall of the Berlusconi cabinet, so as to ascertain how voters have evaluated the current economic and political situation, assessed key political actors, and attributed blame and praise during this cycle. The following analysis stems from an ITANES online five-wave panel study conducted between spring 2011 and winter 2013.

3.   Political Elites and Public Opinion in Times of Political and Economic Turbulence (2011–2013)

In the 2008 election, the centre-right coalition led by Silvio Berlusconi prevailed in a landslide. It replaced a rowdy centre-left government by winning the popular support of 46.3% of the valid votes, and obtaining an absolute majority of seats in both parliamentary chambers. Before contesting the election, the two major parties of the centre-right (Berlusconi's "Go Italy", and Mr Fini's post-fascist National Alliance) joined a new single list – the People of Freedom (PoF) – to match an analogous move by the centre-left, which had created in 2007 the Democratic Party as the common house of former left-leaning Christian Democrats and formerly moderate communists (Bellucci, 2008).

After the victorious election, with Berlusconi as new premier and Fini appointed speaker of the lower parliamentary chamber, the party was formally constituted in March 2009. The cohabitation between the two political components of the coalition soon proved to be uneasy due to differences in policy outlook and direct competition between the two leaders. Berlusconi's "personal party" approach to politics – appealing directly to public opinion, suffering internal party dissent, and displaying an intolerance of time-wasting procedural games and the Byzantinism of Italian politics – greatly contrasted with the more traditional "rank and file" formal procedures requested by Fini in the party's internal decision-making. The contrast burst out in several quarrels over innumerable issues, from granting voting rights to immigrants to bio-ethical policies to candidate selection at the European elections. Berlusconi's sexual scandals also entered the intra-party fight when a political scientist, Ms Sofia Ventura, wrote an article on Mr Fini's foundation website denouncing the People of Freedom's attempt to assure a place on the ballot for some young women from show business. This issue was later taken up in an open letter to the daily *La Republica* by Mr Berlusconi's wife, who later filed for divorce.

The disappointing electoral performance of the new party at both the European and regional elections (2009 and 2010 respectively) exacerbated the contrast between Berlusconi and Fini, and stood in contrast to the electoral gains of the other government partner, the populist Northern League. In April 2010, Fini prompted the creation of an autonomous political group in parliament comprised of 34 representatives who had left the party. The centre-right majority in the lower chamber was therefore put at risk, as became clear in a vote of confidence introduced in the house by the opposition later in December, in which Berlusconi prevailed with a slim edge of three votes (314 versus 311, down from a margin of 60 obtained at the inaugural confidence vote).

Disagreements and internal fights within the centre-right government plagued its action, and were mirrored in its approval rate, which plummeted in the polls after an initial surge following the legislative elections. The economic crisis hit the country severely, and the government presided over an economic trend much worse than that experienced by the previous centre-left government: industrial production fell by 20% in January 2009 and kept a negative pace throughout the year, while unemployment in January 2009 passed the 7% threshold and kept rising to 8.8% by the time of the government's resignation in November 2011. The financial crisis translated into a recession (GDP growth was -5.4% in 2009) and, as the government introduced wider welfare provision for the unemployed in order to shield industrial workers from lay-offs – located mainly in north-eastern Italy, the stronghold of the Northern League – Italy's state deficit rose to 5.4% of GDP in 2009, bringing the government debt to a high of 119.1% of GDP (up from 103.7% in 2007, when a budget-conscious centre-left government cut state expenditures).

Although extremely severe, Italy's economic crisis was no worse than that of other Southern European (and Irish) economies. In fact, it was actually less severe, but for the gigantic public debt; however, this had not prevented Italy meeting the EMS criteria for international markets and banks to buy its bonds. The analysis of how and why national and European elites slowly responded to the crisis that menaced not only single economies but the very existence of the Eurozone is still developing (Cotta, 2012). The phases it went through – a) bank crises and economic recession (fall 2008/winter 2009–2010); b) early sovereign debt crises (winter 2009–2010/ summer 2011); c) acceleration of debt crisis and EU response via Sixpack and Fiscal Compact (summer 2011/winter 2011–2012); and d) ECB intervention via the Outright Monetary Transaction (summer 2012) – highlight a differentiated involvement of national and supranational actors within the European elite. Italy's role in attempting to solve the crisis was perceived domestically as marginal because of its premier's alleged (at home) inadequate international standing and a view abroad of his government's limited range of manoeuvring and policy effectiveness. So while Italy was both a target and a source of financial instability, its political role in Europe and its capacity/visibility in defending Italian interests both appeared greatly tarnished.

Indeed, after the Berlusconi government passed two rigorous budget laws in September 2011, which committed Italy to a balanced budget in 2014 (then anticipated to 2013), the outgoing and incoming presidents of the European Central Bank, Jean-Claude Trichet and Mario Draghi, sent the Italian prime minister a letter dictating a government manifesto detailing further and more rigorous actions and financial measures to be undertaken by Italy almost immediately. Italy followed suit, and further amendments to the budget law were presented in parliament. By that time, however, soon after Greece and Ireland, international markets' loss of confidence damaged also Italy's bonds, whose spread vis-à-vis Germany – still at 183 in July – jumped to 372 on 1 October and skyrocketed to 552 in November.[3] As such, the interest rate paid by other Southern European and Irish bonds was higher than Italy's. However, given the sheer size of the Italian debt, it would greatly affect public finances. Most importantly, government approval fell further, matching the trend of dramatically increasing interest rates.

When, on 11 October 2011, the government failed to produce its annual report on state accounts approved by parliament, it was clear that its majority was evaporating. Political events accelerated quickly, and when parliament passed the state accounts bill in a second vote on 8 November, despite being short of the 316 votes required for an absolute majority, Berlusconi went to the Quirinale Palace to inform the President of the Republic of his strongly "requested" decision to step down after the approval of a financial decree to meet ECB demands. The next day, Mario Monti, a professor of economics and former EU commissioner to the internal market and competition, was nominated by the President of Italian Republic *senatore a vita* ("appointed life senator") with the aim to foster an already agreed "exploratory" asking to form a new government. On 13 November 2011, parliament voted for the financial decree with 380 votes and the abstention of the opposition. Berlusconi resigned immediately afterwards.

Mario Monti was sworn in as new premier on 16 November 2011, heading a cabinet of mainly university professors and experts with no party affiliation. Two days later, the new government won a confidence vote 556 to 61. It was the largest majority in the history of Republican Italy, backed by the People of Freedom, the Democratic Party and the Centrist group. On 6 December, a new Monti decree backed by the grand parliamentary coalition cut state expenditures further and raised the retirement age by six years, up to 67, for both men and women. The interest rate spread fell to 358 points. A reform of labour contracts that made it easier for firms to hire and fire workers – the first task on the earlier ECB letter to Berlusconi – was later approved. The spread fell to 281 in March 2012, signalling that the Monti technocratic government – backed by a parliamentary majority comprising the largest former ruling and opposition parties – had regained some confidence in Italy from the international financial system. However, Monti introduced a highly controversial poll tax on housing in the fall of 2012 in order to raise tax revenues; it extended to the first home a tax earlier introduced by the Berlusconi government on property beyond the first house (to be levied starting in 2014). While the DP backed this tax – seen as a sort of progressive patrimonial levy – the PoF denounced it as an attack on private property. In December 2012 – led by the comeback of Silvio Berlusconi as the party leader – the PoF abandoned the grand coalition, provoking early elections in February 2013, which were also contested by Mario Monti's newly created Scelta Civica party (SC), which had since been joined by the centrist Union of Centre.

Over this period, public opinion, not unexpectedly, perceived the deterioration of the economy quite accurately: showing congruence between macro and micro indicators, the share of Italians who negatively evaluated the national economic situation increased by 15 percentage points (up to 89%) between spring 2011 and spring 2012. It was the worst economic evaluation of the decade (see Table 1): in particular, negative evaluations moved up from 45% to 65% between spring and fall 2011 among those who claimed to have voted for the centre-right ruling parties in 2008, showing a great attenuation of the partisan bias observed in the previous wave, to further reach a high of 91% in 2012.

The overall approval of the Berlusconi government dropped between spring and fall 2011: on a 0–10 scale, the average rating fell from 3.5 to 2.9, with a slight decline of the standard deviations (from 2.7 to 2.5), indicating a gradual consolidation of the negative evaluation (see Figure 1). Government approval actually shrank the most among the 2008 centre-right voters, with a drop of 1.3 points, while it remained more stable among opposition parties' voters. Monti's approval – slightly more popular (3.9 in spring 2012) than Berlusconi's the previous year – appeared more balanced across partisan lines, although centre-left voters showed a greater appreciation.

Trust in political institutions also declined during the economic crisis. Italian political culture has been a paradox for comparative scholars for a long time, where high turnout, high membership in mass-based parties and strong ideological polarizations were matched by mass political alienation, perceptions of low political efficacy, cynicism and mistrust in politicians. Such a syndrome of "limited" social capital and extended political disaffection (Segatti, 2006) are attenuated with the unfolding of "normal" alternation of governments after 1994, thus signalling its dependence from public opinion expectations unfulfilled by the political system, rather than exclusively from some sort of "national character". According to an electoral mandate, responsible governments and policy change effectively eased political disaffection. The poor performance of Berlusconi's government and its fall before the statutory end of legislature, matched by the installation of a cabinet staffed by non-elected officials, reinforced traditional mass political traits. Indeed, overall satisfaction with democracy – a traditional indicator of specific support – fell to 21% (computed as the share of Italians who

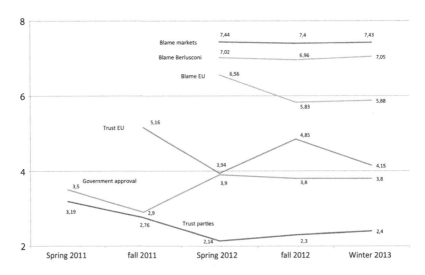

Figure 1. Trend of Italian political attitudes in 2011–2013 (ITANES 2011–2013 Panel)

express much or some satisfaction) at the beginning of 2011, from an average value of 42% in the previous decade (Bellucci & Memoli, 2012); this declined further to 17% in fall 2012, and further again to 12% in spring 2012. Significantly, the panel study shows that it is among the centre-right voters that the drop has been most pronounced (-10 points percentage in fall and -26 points in spring 2012). This obviously reflects the right-wing partisans' disappointment in losing their government (Anderson et al., 2005), but trust in political institutions – as an indicator of legitimacy – also stands at moderate levels. Parties appear to be the least trusted political actors, followed by the parliament, while non-partisan institutions (like the presidency of the Republic, the judiciary and the army) elicit somewhat greater support. The indicator of trust in parties (measured on a 0–10 scale) fell from 3.2 in spring 2011 to 2.1 a year later. Unsurprisingly, although the traditional pro-EU attitude of Italians has waned in recent times, Europe still enjoys a moderate level of trust, although this is clearly declining over time (see Figure 1).

This overall political disaffection of Italian citizens translated over the years into a significant drop in the electoral appeal of the parties, assessed through a measure of the probability to vote (PTV) (van der Eijk et al., 2006). All parties' PTVs fell between 2011 and 2012, with the notable exception of the 5SM, which successfully contested local elections and stood in the polls at 20% of the national vote the month before the election.

When asked to locate the responsibility for Italy's economic crisis, citizens provided a broad image, in which national and international actors share the blame. As indicated by the high mean values of responsibility in spring 2012, the international financial system and the Berlusconi government were perceived as the main culprits (7.4 and 7.0 respectively on a 0–10 scale, which remained stable over the following months). Public opinion seems to reflect rather accurately the public debate on the source of the financial and economic crisis, as well as on the remedies – austerity or fiscal expansion – to cope with it. The balance between national and international responsibilities among public opinion does not follow a direct partisan line, as the narrow variance of the distributions reveal (with the exception of the Berlusconi government). Therefore, both national and supranational governance is singled out. But while the former can be taken for granted both for its relevance and for the partisanship-induced variance of the evaluations, as the "selective attribution" hypothesis suggests (Tilley & Hobolt, 2011), the prominence of the EU appears novel. It is associated in voters' minds with a direct responsibility – i.e. holding a governmental role – and as such, it is exposed to erosion. However, over a six-month period in 2012, the blame on the European Union declined sensibly across all partisans, although the extent to which the European issues have been politicized clearly emerges with unprecedented clarity, acquiring the status of a main political cleavage. Its salience translated into a partisan conflict which promises to be an important determinant of vote choice.[4]

4.   A Model of Vote Choice

In order to explore the determinants of the vote choice (surveyed in the fifth post-election wave), we rely on a multinomial logistic regression, where a vote for the

People of Freedom is taken as the reference category. Following the previous discussion, we test the plausibility of several relevant hypotheses to assess the electoral consequences of the economic crisis: 1) the extent of a (retrospective) economic vote; 2) the structure of blame attribution; and 3) the importance of a (prospective) policy-oriented vote.

All things being equal, interpreting Italians' electoral choices as constituting an economic retrospective vote is a plausible hypothesis. However, both the presence of an outgoing non-partisan government seeking no re-election and an overwhelming negative evaluation of the economy combine to form expectations that economic evaluations will have a weak impact on the vote. The former condition undercuts the reward–punishment perspective (unless the voters choose to focus on the parties in the former elected Berlusconi government), while the latter translates into restricted variance that may render insignificant regression coefficients (Scotto, 2012).

Blame attribution for the crisis is expected to exert a direct effect on parties' appeal and is captured by the hypotheses that centre-right voters would privilege attributing responsibility to non-political actors and to the EU, while left parties' voters would tend to privilege domestic political actors, predominantly the previous Berlusconi government. We expect therefore that centre-right voters might resort to selective blame attribution – singling out the EU or the financial markets – to avoid putting the blame on "their" government, while centre and left voters might rely less on international actors, despite supporters of the radical left appearing weary of the EU and markets. Furthermore, in order to test the globalization hypothesis and the conditioning effect of blame attribution on retrospective economic evaluations, an interaction between retrospective economic concerns and blame attributions is considered, with the expectation that any effect economic evaluation has will be depressed by the attribution of the economic crises to non-governmental/international actors.

We then test the hypothesis of a prospective policy-oriented vote. It is operationalized here via the approval of Monti's government, and through the trust respondents express for the European Union. It could be argued that Monti's approval reflects more valence politics, albeit expressed by competence and leadership, rather than policy preferences. However, the Monti government's public image (and its policy goals) is strongly associated with restoring Italy's finances and the country's standing in the EU; therefore, favouring (opposing) both is assumed as a preference for maintaining (abandoning) the austerity programme developed by the outgoing government – an issue central during the campaign, and which parties strongly disagreed over.

Finally, to control for other important determinants of party preference, left–right self-placement, attitudes towards the poll tax and trust in parties are included in the model, together with standard sociodemographics. To take advantage of the panel design, and to minimize endogeneity bias, left–right self-placement, support for European integration and trust in parties enter the model as observed in the first wave (spring 2011), while all other variables are observed over a year later (in the fourth wave).

The estimates of the multinomial logistic model appear in Table 2. As to the economic vote, the retrospective sociotropic economic evaluation (RSEE) coefficient is only statistically significant for the Democratic Party coalition, and also negatively signed, showing that a perception of a deteriorated economy is associated with a vote for the right bloc rather than for the left one; that is, the associated odds-ratio value (Exp. [b]) shows that the likelihood of a voter perceiving a worsening economy – moving one unit on the 1–3 scale – to vote left rather than right is on average just one-third that of a less economically discontented voter (Exp. [b]: -0.96 = 0.38). This means that the direct effect of economic discontent was to turn on Berlusconi's bloc: an apparent paradoxical outcome given its earlier involvement in government, but which shows the positive impact on voters of the PoF's strategic choice to distance the party from the grand coalition in the last months of the legislature. The only other party which benefits from economic grievances is Grillo's 5SM, although its influence is uncertain given the lack of statistical significance.

The structure of blame attribution confirms our hypotheses: holding the previous Berlusconi government responsible for the crisis clearly and significantly depresses a vote for the former government's coalition parties (PoF and NL), while it boosts the likelihood to vote for extreme leftist parties, the DP, Monti's list and 5SM. On the contrary, finding the culprit in the EU contributes to a preference for the People of Freedom and the Northern League. Likewise, despite widespread popular sentiment, blaming the international financial markets only exerts a negative political impact for the Democratic Party bloc and Monti's one, boosting the likelihood of voting for the PoF; the associated odds-ratio values show that the odds of voting for DP or Monti rather than PoF moved one unit on the 0–10 scale of blame, depresses their vote by an average factor of 23% and 36% respectively (Exp. [b]: -0.26 = 0.77; Exp. [b]: -0.44 = 0.64).

When the RSSE is interacted with blame attribution we see – as expected – a differentiated impact on voters' choice: economically discontented voters who perceive the PoF as responsible for the crisis are 1.6 times more likely to vote for DP rather than Berlusconi's bloc (Exp. [B]: 0.49= 1.63), thus balancing the negative direct effect of the economic grievance on the left vote. The interaction of economic grievances with blaming the EU for the crises is also interesting. While the direct impact of blaming the EU ("Blame EU for crisis") favours the PoF – as we have seen – the interactions show a positive effect on all the votes for the other parties vis-à-vis Berlusconi's bloc. This means that – contrary to our expectations – when voters associate economic downturns with supranational European governance, they are more likely to choose parties which take a pro-Europe stance, rather than those openly Eurosceptic – albeit with different intensities.

Turning to policy voting, the indicators of Monti's government approval and support for the EU show a rather weak impact. Pro-European attitudes are significant only in the contrast between a vote for the extreme left and the PoF bloc, while government approval only positively impacts the Monti list vote. Finally, attitudes

Table 2. Multinomial logistic model of vote choice, 2013 (logit coefficients and std.err. in brackets; base category: People of Freedom Coalition – PoF+ Northern League-)

	Extreme left	Democratic Party Coalition (DP+SEL)	Monti Coalition (SC + UDC)	Five Stars Movement (5SM)	Other parties
Retrospective sociotropic economic evaluation – RSEE $_{t-1}$	−0.67 (1.19)	−0.96 (0.51)*	−0.51 (0.61)	0.28 (0.55)	−0.16 (0.66)
Blame Berlusconi government for crisis $_{t-1}$	0.62 (0.34)*	0.36 (0.15)**	0.32 (0.18)*	0.60 (0.14)***	0.21 (0.17)
Blame EU for crisis $_{t-1}$	−0.53 (0.25)**	−0.29 (0.15)**	−0.42 (0.17)**	−0.34 (0.14)**	0.03 (0.19)
Blame international financial markets for crisis $_{t-1}$	−0.22 (0.28)	−0.26 (0.16)*	−0.44 (0.21)**	−0.18 (0.14)	−0.05 (0.20)
RSEE x Blame Berlusconi	0.05 (0.63)	0.49 (0.28)*	0.32 (0.35)	−0.11 (0.24)	0.26 (0.32)
RSEE x Blame EU	0.72 (0.44)*	0.46 (0.27)*	0.68 (0.31)**	0.63 (0.26)**	−0.31 (0.34)
RSEE x Blame markets	0.20 (0.59)	0.20 (0.31)	0.24 (0.24)	−0.05 (0.29)	0.34 (0.42)
Left–right self-placement $_{t-4}$	−0.99 (0.03)***	−0.88 (0.10)***	−0.23 (0.11)**	−0.41 (0.09)***	−0.24 (0.02)**
Support EU integration $_{t-4}$	0.37 (0.17)**	0.06 (0.07)	0.08 (0.09)	0.03 (0.07)	0.20 (0.10)**
Government approval $_{t-1}$	−0.07 (0.19)	0.13 (0.11)	0.89 (0.17)***	−0.13 (0.11)	0.28 (0.03)
Trust parties $_{t-4}$	0.56 (1.37)	−0.81 (0.63)	0.68 (0.84)	1.81 (0.65)**	0.17 (0.75)
House tax $_{t-1}$	0.12 (0.77)	−0.83 (0.43)*	0.07 (0.51)	−0.51 (0.42)	0.68 (0.56)
Social Class	0.85 (0.41)**	0.21 (0.21)	0.24 (0.26)	0.11 (0.20)	−0.07 (0.27)
Gender	2.7 (0.95)***	0.23 (0.44)	1.1 (0.55)**	0.65 (0.41)	−0.10 (0.57)

Education	−0.25 (0.66)	−0.17 (0.37)	0.74 (0.46)*	−0.32 (0.34)	0.14 (0.43)
Religion	−1.49 (0.70)**	−0.13 (0.29)	−0.27 (0.35)	−0.57 (0.27)**	−0.38 (0.35)
Age	0.07 (0.59)	−0.53 (0.31)*	−0.68 (0.39)*	−1.01 (0.29)***	−0.81 (0.38)**
Constant	−2.29 (6.7)	11.38 (3.01)***	−3.26 (3.6)	4.17 (3.01)	−2.59 (3.90)
LR Chi2 (85)	624.70				
Pseudo R2 (N. cases)	0.46 (477)				

Notes: *** $p < 0.01$; ** $p < 0.05$; * $p < 0.10$

Definition of variables: "Vote choice" is reported vote to the lower house in the post-electoral panel wave (T0); "RSEE" is respondent evaluation of the country's economic situation over the last year, coded 1 = improved, 2 = stayed the same, 3 = worsened; "Blame Berlusconi government for crisis" is the respondent's responsibility attribution on a 0–10 scale; "Blame EU for crisis" is the respondent's responsibility attribution on a 0–10 scale; "Blame international financial markets for crisis" is the respondent's responsibility attribution on a 0–10 scale; "Blame Berlusconi", "Blame EU" and "Blame markets" interacted with RSEE are recoded in dummy variables (values => 6 are coded 1, other values =0); "Left–right self-placement" is respondent's position on a 0–10 scale; "Support EU integration" is respondent's position on a 0–10 scale from "some say European Union's unification has already gone too far" to "European unification should be further strengthened"; "Government approval" is respondent's evaluation on a 0–10 scale; "Trust parties": 0= yes, 1= no; "House tax": 1= keep as it is, 2= to be reduced, 3= to be abolished; "Social class" is respondent or household head's profession: 1= service; 2= routine non-manual, 3= self-employed; 4= manual workers; "Gender": 1= male, 2= female; "Education": 1= elementary, 2= high school, 3= university; "Religion" is church attendance: 1= never, 2= seldom, 3= weekly; "Age": 1= 18–34; 2=35–54, 3 = > 54. T-1 variables and T-4 variables are observed respectively in the fourth and first of the five-wave panel.

towards parties ("Trust Parties") clearly and strongly affect voting for 5SM: the odds of voting for Grillo's movement are six times greater than for the PoF among voters who distrust parties than among those who do not (Exp. [b]: $1.81 = 6.1$), thus showing that anti-party sentiment was the strongest drive of the 5SM vote. Similarly, opposing the house tax was a significant predictor of the PoF vote, depressing by a factor of more than half the likelihood to vote for DP among voters who opposed the new levy (Exp. [b]: $-0.83 = 0.43$)

Finally, we observe how the vote probabilities change according to a unit change of selected independent variables if all others are held at their mean value. This allows us to assess their marginal effects – expressed as the change in the probability to vote for each party based on the model of Table 2 – thus rendering comparison of each variable's impact on vote choice more straightforward with respect to the odds-value previously reported. The direct effect of retrospective sociotropic economic evaluations (RSEE) clearly penalizes the DP (-27%), while it moderately favours the PoF (+2%). Interacting RSSE and blaming the EU for the crisis significantly boosts the 5SM vote (+5%), while the interaction between RSSE and "Blame Berlusconi for the economic crisis" improves the probability of a DP vote (+9%) and depresses that for the PoF (-2%). These effects are graphically displayed in Figure 2, which due to space constraints focuses only on the PD vote versus a vote for the PoF. The direct marginal effect (displayed are also the 95% confidence intervals) of the RSEE negatively impacts moving from a positive to a pessimist evaluation of the national economy (Figure 2, Panel A). However, holding the EU responsible for the crisis further reduces the likelihood to vote for the Democratic Party over the People of Freedom among discontented voters: the conditional effect of EU blame attribution shows a reduction of the probability to vote DP the greater EU responsibility is assessed (Figure 2, Panel B). On the other hand, blaming Berlusconi for the crisis moderately improves the likelihood of a DP vote among voters with a negative evaluation of the state of the economy (Figure 2, Panel C).

Summing up, this analysis shows that controlling for traditional vote determinants, the public's perception of whom to blame for the economic crisis has been electorally consequential. In other words, holding national or supranational institutions responsible carries relevant weight for the vote choice. Retrospective economic evaluations have exerted a moderate direct effect on voting in 2013, negatively affecting the Democratic Party. But we have also shown that the influence of people's retrospective economic assessments on their choice is conditional on a perception of responsibility attribution; therefore, holding the former party in government responsible turns voters to the main left party, whereas voters support the former government leader when this mediation is missing. Similarly, economic discontent associated with blame attribution to the EU does not move voters towards Eurosceptical parties, but demonstrates a demand for more European governance. Italian public opinion seems to have been aware of the political importance of the economic crisis, and to be responsive to the ways parties frame this issue.

1-A. Marginal effects of economic evaluation on the DP coalition vote (with 95% CIs)

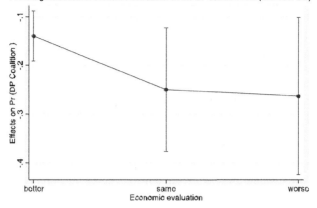

1-B. Conditional effects of EU blame attribution on the DP Coalition vote (with 95% CIs)

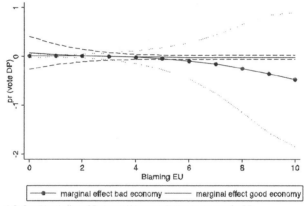

1-C. Conditional effect of Berlusconi blame attribution on the vote for DP Coalition vote (with 95% CIs)

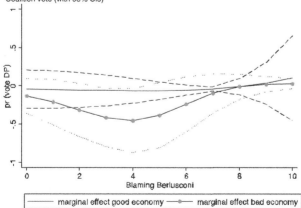

Figure 2. Conditional effects of blame attribution and retrospective economic evaluation on the vote for the Democratic Party Coalition

5. Conclusions

The (partially) unexpected fall of the government headed by Silvio Berlusconi in 2011 tarnished the most representative political figure of the centre-right. Berlusconi's reputation and that of his party for managing the economy were much more severely damaged by the loss of confidence by the international markets than by his sexual misconduct. The choice not to call a new election, but to install a President of the Republic's government in which parties did not play a direct role, was apparently successful. The main parties' strategy to distance themselves from a government intent on harsh fiscal policies and welfare cuts while supporting it in parliament may be seen as a Machiavellian stratagem to elude voters' blame. The resignation of the Monti government in December 2012 – following the comeback of Berlusconi and the withdrawal of his support for the grand coalition government – opened a political campaign that centred on the austerity measures dictated by European institutions. The analysis of this article shows that citizens' economic pessimism was not devoid of a clear understanding of the performance of political actors, as suggested by their use of this information to orient their vote choice. The electoral results – showing the largest swing-vote in the history of the Italian Republic – produced a hung parliament, and forced the main left- and right-wing parties to unite in another grand coalition. Voters' behaviour highlights that the great success of the 5SM was not due to retrospective economic discontent, but rather to mistrust of the traditional political actors. Of course, economic distress affected voters' choice, but partisans assigned responsibility differently, according to their perceptions of the main culprits. Economic voting was therefore mediated by the structure of blame attribution.

Funding

Research for this article has been supported by Ministry of Education PRIN grants N. 20083P4BYT (2008) and N. 2010943X4L_012 (2010-11).

Notes

1. Berlusconi's first cabinet in 1994 lasted only eight months due to the withdrawal of its minor partner, the Northern League, from the government coalition. After a term with the opposition, the centre-right pre-electoral alliance, he had again forged a win at the 2001 election and stayed in power ever since (but for the brief 2006–2008 centre-left government led by Romano Prodi).
2. The ITANES inter-electoral panel study was conducted via online interviews with a representative sample of the adult population with Internet access (recruited by the polling agency SWG) as part of an experimental study on the impact of survey modes comparing telephone and online interviews. The survey was administered in spring 2011, fall 2011, spring 2012, fall 2012 and winter 2013. Of the initial sample (N=1,500), 61% of respondents (N=908) completed all five waves.
3. A spread of 100 points means that the interest on ten years' worth of government bonds is 1% higher than the interest rate paid on German bonds.
4. The heightened salience of the EU issue is revealed by the correlation between government approval and EU trust: it was small (-0.05) at the time of the Berlusconi government (fall 2012), but increased to 0.5 with Monti in 2012.

References

Anderson, C.J. (2007) The end of economic voting? Contingency dilemmas and the limits of democratic accountability. *Annual Review of Political Science*, 10, pp. 271–296.

Anderson, C.J. & Hecht, J.D. (2012) When the economy goes bad, everyone is in charge, and no one is to blame: the case of the 2009 German election. *Electoral Studies*, 31(1), pp. 5–19.

Anderson, C.J., Blais, A., Bowler, S., Donovan, T. & Listaug, O. (2005) *Losers' Consent: Elections and Democratic Legitimacy* (Oxford: Oxford University Press).

Bellucci, P. (2008) Why Berlusconi's landslide return? A comment on the 2008 Italian general election. *PVS Politische ViertelJahresschrift*, 49(4), pp. 605–617.

Bellucci, P. (2012) Government accountability and vote choice in Italy: 1990–2008. *Electoral Studies*, 31(3), pp. 491–497.

Bellucci, P. & Conti, N. (eds) (2012) *Gli italiani e l'Europa. Opinione pubblica, élite politiche e media* (Rome: Carocci).

Bellucci, P. & Memoli, V. (2012) The determinants of democratic satisfaction in Europe, in: D. Sanders, P.C. Magalhães & G. Toka (eds) *Citizens and the European Polity: Mass Attitudes towards the European and National Polities* (Oxford: Oxford University Press), pp. 9–38.

Bellucci, P.M., Costa Lobo, M. & Lewis-Beck, M. (2012) Economic crisis and elections: the European periphery. *Electoral Studies*, 31(3), pp. 469–471.

Chiaramonte, A. & Emanuele, V. (2013) Volatile e tripolare: il nuovo sistema politico Italiano, in: L. De Sio, M. Cataldi & F. De Lucia (eds) *Le elezioni politiche 2013* (Rome: Luiss University Press), pp. 95–100.

Clarke, H., Sanders, D., Stewart, M. & Whiteley, P. (2009) *Performance Politics and the British Voter* (Oxford: Oxford University Press).

Costa Lobo, M. & Lewis-Beck, M.S. (2012) The integration hypothesis: how the European Union shapes economic voting. *Electoral Studies*, 31(3), pp. 522–528.

Cotta, M. (2012) Facing the crisis: the variable geometry of the European elite system and its effects. Paper presented to *Elites and Trans-Atlantic Crisis: A Symposium*, University of Texas at Austin, 2–4 April.

Cutler, F. (2008) Whodunnit? Voters and responsibility in Canadian federalism. *Canadian Journal of Political Science/Revue canadienne de science politique*, 41(3), pp. 627–654.

de Vries, C.E. (2007) Sleeping giant: fact or fairytale? How European elections affects national elections. *European Union Politics*, 8(3), pp. 363–385.

Duch, R.M. & Stevenson, R. (2008) *The Economic Vote: How Political and Economic Institutions Condition Election Results* (Cambridge: Cambridge University Press).

Duch, R.M. & Stevenson, R. (2010) The global economy, competency, and the economic vote. *The Journal of Politics*, 72(1), pp. 105–123.

van der Eijk, C., van der Brug, W., Kroh, M. & Franklin, M. (2006) Rethinking the dependent variable in voting behavior: on the measurement and analysis of electoral utilities. *Electoral Studies*, 25(3), pp. 424–447.

Evans, G. & Pickup, M. (2010) Reversing the causal arrow: the political conditioning of economic perceptions in the 2000–2004 US presidential election cycle. *The Journal of Politics*, 72(4), pp. 1236–1251.

Fernandez-Albertos, J. (2006) Does internationalisation blur responsibility? Economic voting and economic openness in 15 European countries. *Western European Politics*, 29(1), pp. 28–46.

Fiske, S.T. & Taylor, S.E. (1991) *Social Cognition*, 2nd edn (New York, USA: McGraw-Hill).

Hellwig, T. (2008) Globalization, policy constraints, and the vote choice. *The Journal of Politics*, 70(4), pp. 1128–1141.

Hobolt, S., Tilley, J. & Wittrock, J. (2013) Listening to the government: how information shapes responsibility attributions. *Political Behavior*, 35(1), pp. 153–174.

Lewis-Beck, M.S. & Paldam, M. (2000) Economic voting: an introduction. *Electoral Studies*, 19(2–3), pp. 113–121.

Lewis-Beck, M. & Stegmaier, M. (2007) Economic models of voting, in: R. Dalton & H.-D. Klingemann (eds) *The Oxford Handbook of Political Behavior* (Oxford, Oxford University Press), pp. 518–537.

Magalhães, P. (2012) After the bailout: responsibility, policy, and valence in the Portuguese legislative election of June 2011. *South European Society and Politics*, 17(2), pp. 309–327.

Rudolph, T.J. (2003) Who's responsible for the economy? The formation and consequences of responsibility attributions. *American Journal of Political Science*, 47(4), pp. 698–713.

Scotto, T.J. (2012) Conclusion: thinking about models of economic voting in hard times. *Electoral Studies*, 31(3), pp. 529–531.

Segatti, P. (2006) Italy, forty years of political disaffection, in: M. Torcal & J.R. Montero (eds) *Political Disaffection in Contemporary Democracies: Social Capital, Institutions, and Politics* (London and New York, Routledge) pp. 244–275.

Stokes, D. (1992) Valence politics, in: D. Kavanagh (ed.) *Electoral Politics* (Oxford: Clarendon Press), pp. 141–164.

Tilley, J. & Hobolt, S.B. (2011) Is the government to blame? An experimental test of how partisanship shapes perceptions of performance and responsibility. *The Journal of Politics*, 73(2), pp. 1–15.

Appendix

Table A1. Results of legislative elections in Italy, 2008–2013

	House, 2008			House, 2013			Senate, 2008			Senate, 2013		
	Votes	%	Seats	Votes	%	Seats	Votes	%	Seats	Votes	%	Seats
Democratic Party	12,424,536	33.1	217	8,932,615	25.5	297	11,369,735	33.1	118	8,683,690	27.0	109
Sel				1,106,784	3.1	37				912,308	2.8	7
Other parties	1,664,432		30	313,876	0.9	11	1,634,443	4.8	16	666,852	2.1	7
DP Coalition	*14,088,968*	*37.5*	*247*	*10,353,275*	*29.5*	*345*	*13,002,178*	*37.9*	*134*	*10,262,850*	*31.9*	*123*
People of Freedom	13,957,323	37.2	276	7,478,796	21.3	98	12,994,510	37.8	147	6,965,639	21.7	98
Northern League	3,027,080	8.1	60	1,392,398	4.0	18	2,644,247	7.7	25	1,331,163	4.1	17
Other parties	410,487	1.1	8	1,202,915	3.4	9	355,076	1.0	2	1,342,024	4.2	2
PoF Coalition	*17,394,890*	*46.4*	*344*	*10,074,109*	*28.7*	*125*	*15,993,833*	*46.6*	*174*	*9,638,826*	*30.0*	*117*
Monti List (SC)				3,004,739	8.6	39				2,984,128	9.3	19
Other parties				768,897	2.2	8						
Monti Coalition				*3,773,636*	*10.8*	*47*						
5SM				8,797,902	25.1	109				7,471,671	23.2	54
Lists outside coalitions	6,056,439	16.1	39	2,058,365	5.6	4	5,329,648	15.5	7	1,766,506	5.5	2
Total	37,540,297	100	630	35,057,287	100	630	34,325,659	100	315	32,123,981	100	315
Turnout		80.5			75.2			80.5			75.2	

Source: Ministry of Interior.

Index

Note: Pages numbers in *italics* represent tables
Page numbers in **bold** represent figures
Page numbers followed by 'n' refer to notes

For Product Safety Concerns and Information please contact our EU
representative GPSR@taylorandfrancis.com Taylor & Francis Verlag GmbH,
Kaufingerstraße 24, 80331 München, Germany

Printed and bound by CPI Group (UK) Ltd, Croydon, CR0 4YY
01/05/2025
01858452-0006